# WOMEN OF VISION:

## Ordinary Women, Extraordinary Lives

*Kathleen Smith & Elizabeth Ireland*

**Outskirts Press, Inc.**
**Denver, Colorado**

Outskirts Press, Inc.
http://www.outskirtspress.com

ISBN: 978-1-4327-3187-8

Library of Congress Control Number: 2008934373

Outskirts Press and the "OP" logo are trademarks belonging to Outskirts Press, Inc.

PRINTED IN THE UNITED STATES OF AMERICA

We dedicate this book to our magnificent sisters


Leslie Smith Lantis
Jean McCormick Petty

# *Acknowledgments*

Ralph Waldo Emerson once said: "Every great achievement is a triumph of enthusiasm." This was certainly true for us, as this journey has been one of unfolding joy.

We had some very enthusiastic support from those with whom we came into contact during the creation of this book and would like to acknowledge the contribution of the women we met and interviewed who have been incredibly helpful, supportive, and generous. It is our hope to be a small part of their vision and purpose and that you enjoy reading about these extraordinary women.

We wish to thank our Advisory Council: Kathleen Ryan, Deb Samuel, Tricia Molloy, Jan Dahlin Geiger, Janine Bolon, Barbara Stanny, and Therra Gwynn. We are so grateful for their support, wisdom, and loving criticism.

We recognize the support of our friends and family as they encouraged us on this path. Liz would particularly like to thank her incredible friends Paula Keenan, for always being there for her, even when Paula thinks she's crazy, and Mona Lyden Moore, who taught her how to write with a partner with love and great humor. She also wants to thank her family; her most considerate and loving husband, Jay, her beloved daughter, Mai Lan, and her indomitable mother-in-law, Louise. Kathleen would like to thank friends and family who gave much support during the past eighteen months — her beloved aunt, Barbara Manning, brother, Michael Smith; friends Glenda Ryan and Gloria Dunham; Bonnie Long, at whose Tybee Island home the first draft was begun; Carole O'Connell, who provided incredible guidance to launch a new life; and an oh-so-supportive brother-in-law, Bob Lantis. We both also wish to thank Patty Mosteller and Pat Masotti for their continuing advice and marketing suggestions.

The genesis for this book came from an idea that was sparked by author Mary Manin Morrissey, *Building Your Field of Dreams*, keynote speaker at a women's retreat we attended. We are grateful for her abundant wisdom and authenticity.

We appreciate the help of Laura Young and everyone at Outskirts Press who worked on our behalf, on a very hectic timeline.

Our own vision for *Women of Vision* is much larger than this book. It is only the beginning. You can contact us at: www.womenofvisionproject.com with your ideas. We encourage all the women who read this book to step out with your ideas, release and claim the extraordinary within, and fully become the woman of vision that you truly are meant to be.

# Contents

# *Foreword*

We are two women who, for a very long time, have wanted to do a creative project together. We have known each other for over twenty years and consider ourselves soul sisters. We have shared a number of adventures together, involving everything from travel to foreign countries to business investments — none of which were exactly the right fit for us. However, that never deterred us in our quest to find that perfect project to complement our talents and friendship.

Kathleen had dreamed of writing a book since college. But life intervened, and after college she found herself developing a career in communications. After spending over fifteen years traveling the country for companies such as The Weather Channel and Walt Disney Company, she became VP of Communications and Center Initiatives at the Woodruff Arts Center in Atlanta in 2001. There she wrote extensively; trade articles and op-ed pieces, annual reports, foundation grant proposals, as well as the composition of many senior executive speeches. Exciting as all that was, she still longed to pen her own project. She and Liz formed a partnership in late 2006 to do just that, and in early 2007 Kathleen was ready to place her career on hold and dedicate her time to researching the book with Liz.

Liz found her passion for the theater at an early age. After finishing graduate school, she embarked upon a career as an instructor in the performing arts center of a liberal arts college in northern Illinois. For ten years she taught, directed, and managed house operations for a vibrant performing arts program and wrote or re-wrote a number of plays. She lived, breathed, and celebrated in her theatrical life. Soon after receiving tenure and an associate professorship, she realized she had been chewed up and spit out by her dedication, and grasped at the chance to take a well-deserved sabbatical. In no time at all, she discovered that theater no longer held the fascination for her it once had. Today she attends the theater occasionally, most often to celebrate in the performance of her friends. However, she did rediscover a passion for writing and turned her talents to screenwriting, eventually writing fifteen screenplays either by herself or with partners. Two of her own scripts were semifinalists for the *Don and Gee Nicholl Fellowship* in screenwriting, sponsored by the Academy of Motion Picture Arts and Sciences, while four others were optioned, but remain unproduced. As primary caregiver for her ninety-three-year-old mother-in-law and beautiful adopted eleven-year-old Chinese daughter, she now sees herself as the heroine in her *own* comedy-adventure film.

The turning point came for both of us during the fall of 2006 when we attended a women's retreat held outside of Atlanta (something we highly recommend all women of vision do, if nothing else for the sake of personal renewal). We were at beautiful Callaway Gardens when we first came in contact with the keynote speaker, Mary Manin Morrissey. Author of a number of books, including *Building Your Field of Dreams*, Mary spoke to all of us about "What Every Woman Can Be" and how every woman is a woman of vision.

Aha! That was a defining moment for us. It started us thinking about why that was so and how it could be expressed. Then we started thinking about all the wonderful accomplishments so many women have and are achieving and the positive effect they make. We wanted to seek out and uncover the lives of women who have awakened to their power, discovered their purpose, and merged it with their ingenuity to empower others and impact the world in a positive way.

It was our original intention to celebrate those women that all of us know — those everyday women, those ordinary *she-roes* who with grace, passion, and courage use their intuition to create a life of vision. We know there are so many of these women, of all ages and all walks of life. We had the opportunity to meet many who wish to use their lives in ways to better our world, for their families, their children, their friends, and everyone around them.

While we are all familiar with the well-known names of those who create this kind of life, certainly Mother Teresa, Princess Diana, Oprah Winfrey, Melinda Gates, and numerous others we could mention, we are also aware of ordinary women in each of our lives who achieve extraordinary things. It was there that our interest lay. We figured there had to be a lot of women who were living their dreams. We believed these women were just about everywhere. They just didn't get much press.

We set out to find them, interview them, and discover what commonalities they had. It soon became apparent to us that a part of *our* vision could also be about helping these women to achieve *their* vision by celebrating them in our book. We also thought if we could offer a little inspiration to other women who were looking to express their dreams, we could do it through the exploration of who these women are and what they are doing. Along the way, we could offer a little practical guidance and a gentle push to help others launch their dream. So, that's how we gave birth to *Women of Vision: Ordinary Women, Extraordinary Lives.*

We got off to a slow start. We were well prepared, we knew the kind of women we were looking for, and we were organized. There was only one tiny problem. *We had no idea how we were going to attract the women we were looking for or get them to agree to an interview with us.*

We started with the women we knew. We let everyone know what we were looking for — and it started to build. It seemed when we began to search for these women, they were just about everywhere. It was very exciting. We see, hear, and read so much bad press about when some women go wrong, but we so rarely hear about the great things the majority of women are doing. It seemed we couldn't talk to anyone without that person recommending or referring us to someone she knew who fit our target. We would pick up a magazine, and there in the back would be a small story about a woman who was making a positive impact on the world around her. It was almost as if when we decided to *look* for these women, they were attracted to *us*!

We found Kate Atwood and *Kate's Club* in the back of *People Magazine* and through a personal reference. We found Becky Douglas and *Rising Star Outreach* through an acquaintance of hers Liz met at a garage sale. Barbara Duffy's daughter heard about what we were doing and contacted us about her mother. Sisters told us about their sisters. Mothers told us about their daughters. Daughters told us about their mothers. Liz's daughter's piano teacher suggested

Serena Woolrich and the online community she has created for survivors of the Holocaust and their children at www.allgenerations.org. Kathleen found Wendy Daly when she heard her salon was the only one in town that carried the products Kathleen prefers. Kathleen walked in and found Wendy and her initiative, *Indigo Sky*. And each woman we interviewed would recommend others and, in many cases, provide us an introduction.

These are the women who have found a path, a way to bring more light into so many people's lives. These women truly represent us all, the younger and older generations, black, white; all the myriad of diverse cultures. What all have in common is a desire to change some part of the world for the better, to create a positive force. That and the fact that the vast majority of them don't seek fame or have the media proclaiming their life events to the world; they simply live their lives and include in it some remarkable methods of touching others.

These women are your sisters, aunts, cousins, neighbors, or your mothers. It could be your best friend who sees a need in the community, feels a passion to fill it, then devises a way to do just that. Right now it may be you. We are all within six degrees of separation from that woman.

The interview process was really a gift to us. We met many amazing women. What really stood out in all the interviews was how giving, how generous all the women were to us. They were so anxious to help us, to give to us. We were struck by how busy they all were, yet also how happy and just plain *jazzed* they were.

As Becky Douglas, *Rising Star Outreach,* put it: "I get up at five or six o'clock, and I hit the floor running. I'm already behind, and I go until twelve or one in the morning, and I don't know why I'm not dead because I just keep running, running, running, and I'm always behind. But there's an energy that comes when you help people. I don't know how to describe it…because I don't go to sleep exhausted. I go to sleep easily."

Then we started thinking about what, if anything, bound these women together. Even though they lived in different parts of the country and were interested in different things, what common thread ran through their lives? We found it was their conscious decision, at some point in their lives, to speak what we have come to term the "I will." Are there two more powerful words in the English language? "I will." I will serve my family, my church, my community, my school, my passion, my country, and in so doing, I will serve myself.

That is the inspiration and purpose for this book. Our hope is to reach women everywhere, in all walks of life, inspiring them with the true stories of the women we found. We seek to provide some direction that those of you who have found your way to this book can then choose to follow, or blaze your own trail. It was Monica Willard, of the United Religions Initiative, United Nations NGO Representative (non-governmental organization) and advocate for a culture of peace, who prophesized our journey for us: "I don't know what it takes for you to make this kind of shift in your life. But you're going to meet some interesting people, and you're also able to follow your heart's desire." It is true for her, for every woman we spoke with, and it certainly became true for us.

We next asked ourselves, what if these women of vision could reach out and touch all of us; both inspire and guide us, as we seek to pursue our own dreams? What might happen next? This book celebrates some women who have chosen to say: "I will." We think there are many, many more: perhaps tens of thousands of women who make that commitment every day.

A few of the examples of women we encountered, and you'll soon meet, who live lives of significance include:

**Kate Atwood**, I will create a place where grieving children can heal.

**Becky Douglas,** I will eradicate leprosy by 2022.

**Serena Woolrich,** I will provide a source of communication, information, and connection to Holocaust survivors, their families, historians, and filmmakers.

**Carole O'Connell,** I will show people how to create joy in their lives.

**Monica Willard,** I will make a stand for peace in the world.

**Heidi Kuhn**, I will turn minefields into vineyards all over the world.

**Jan Dahlin Geiger**, I will make money fun.

You, too, are a woman of vision. We know you are because you have picked up this book, and on some level it speaks to you.

We started our interviews by asking the same questions of

everyone. While we had a set of questions that asked what we wanted to know, we thought they would lead us in very similar directions. We were wrong. Each individual woman had her own story, and in sharing it, led us on many different journeys. These women became our teachers, and we are so grateful for the wisdom they imparted to us.

We expected to be moved by the lives of these women and continually found ourselves touched by their individual experiences. More than once we shed tears together over the story of their journeys. However, we have to say that we spent much more time laughing because of the pure joy these women expressed in what they do and what they shared with us. It was such a gift.

We encourage you all, when you encounter whatever it is that moves you, to take that step forward and say "I will" and choose a life of significance. You, too, can demonstrate that a single person can make a better world and lead the way for a new generation.

We hope the stories we are about to share with you will allow you to be inspired so that you will aspire to do the same. Also, if this book helps you to find an expression in your life, please let us know. We love hearing from all the women of vision out there and where they are on achieving their dreams.

You can reach us through: www.womenofvisionproject.com

Kathleen Smith
Elizabeth Ireland

# *Introduction*

Welcome to our world. If you look around, you might think it has some real problems. Problems that governments or militaries cannot solve. Problems that politicians cannot, or will not solve. So people do. Ordinary people, like you and me. You are about to meet some of them and learn how they discovered a passion within themselves, and followed it, to become a light in this world for so many people, in order to solve their problems.

## Agents of Social Change

And, importantly, these people are women. They turned themselves loose to solve those problems, with their passion and their vision. They are so much more able to do this than any government, military, or politician. Kathy Headlee, founder and head of *Mothers Without Borders,* put it succinctly recently in her interview with us. "Women are agents of social change."

If you are a mother, you are an agent of social change. If you volunteer in any capacity, you are an agent of change. If you have a job in any work or office environment where you interact daily with others, you are an agent of social change. You have beliefs that you expound upon with others, you feel things deeply as a woman, and you want things to be better and better, to have all those around you feel joy. You are truly an agent of social change.

You may never have realized this; the power you hold within can bring about change. The women in this book did, as did many others like them. That is the only difference between them and you. They are women who have awakened to their power. They are conscious of it; their vision is focused and fueled by their passion. They consciously use all at their command to bring about change, improve the lives of so many, and enlighten our world in the process.

All over the world people — women — are capable of solving their own problems, but they need resources to do it. This book is such a resource.

## Why Women

Women's identity and self-esteem have historically been generated by their relationships and associations. Conversely, men have received most of their identity and self-esteem from the outer world, through jobs, income, accomplishments, and accolades. Today's women — especially those in America — are feeling primed to explore their outer world and are uniquely qualified to bring a new perspective long missing.

Throughout most of our history, the vast majority of women died by their forties. And those who lived longer could expect to experience physical decline.

Today, a woman's life expectancy is eighty-four, and most women will experience these years with vibrancy, a sharp mind, and more influence. This is the greatest time in history to be a woman, especially if you live in developed countries such as the United States and England. We have the incredible luck to both be women AND be alive in this time.

Being a woman usually means having a deep, unending reserve of compassion, an incredible energy resource culled down through time by our need to multitask; holding both our families and households together while maintaining a high level of diplomacy with all those who would try to rule us. Now, with our incredible freedom having evolved, our abilities and energy can be matched with our innate womanhood, allowing us to utilize our talents once reserved for home and hearth to bear on areas we feel passionate about in our world. Women around the world are assuming the role of saving our very planet and civilization.

# Woman Evolving

A shift has begun in our world, especially in those areas of the world known as "first world" countries. This change began in the twentieth century and is now reaching the tipping point. It involves the role of women in our civilization, a role that in the past has seen our talents and particular traits forced into a very narrow realm. This role was not a minor one, that of bearing and nurturing the family, but our very traits and abilities were never keenly respected by those in authority. Thus our talent and passion were not utilized in ways that might have had a greater impact on our developing civilization. Our "personal touch" might have been brought to bear on the conflicts that were a constant in our world's history, and provided vital missing support to those fringes of our society.

Can you name ten historical women who followed their passion and contributed to the betterment of their world? Can you come up with a few, at least one or two, but others elude you? How many of those you just thought of were later denigrated or (yikes) burned at a stake? History has not been kind to women who attempted to step out of their designated roles and follow their own vision to influence their world.

This was not done consciously to remove a nurturing attitude from the world. It was done primarily through ignorance, and perhaps a form of narcissism by men primarily, of the value of the female psyche. Women, at varying times, have been as lowly viewed as outright property, or a lesser being of reduced intelligence. As recently as the late 1800s, philosopher Herbert Spencer stated that thinking was dangerous for females. "The overtaxing of their brains," he declared, "would lead to the deficiency of reproductive power." This was a common assumption based on the latest scientific studies of the day. So women were forbidden or merely limited by the laws and social dictates of their environment.

But our female forebears still managed to leave a mark on many people worldwide. Most are not now, nor ever will be, widely known. Their gender and their place in time warranted their shunting to the rear and out of recorded history. They must be represented by the few who managed to stand out and be noticed, many times to their detriment. That is how we know of them now. Women like

England's Gertrude Bell, the "Queen of the Desert," who defied the established mores of England's Victorian age to become one of the first women educated through Oxford, and then spent a life in support of the people of Mesopotamia, eventually helping lead the formation of the Arab states, especially the creation of Iraq.

American Clara Barton, a nurse during the Civil War, became the "lady in charge" of the hospitals at the front. Clara ultimately launched a nationwide campaign for President Lincoln to identify missing soldiers from the Civil War, tracing the fate of thirty thousand men. She is most known for lobbying Congress to launch Europe's International Committee of the Red Cross in America, later expanding the American Red Cross to respond to crises in any national disaster.

Significant changes in the view and "rights" of women began to accelerate in the twentieth century, ultimately exploding in several countries, especially in North America and Europe, during the latter half of the century. Women began to explore roles outside of the home, expanding their role in their communities.

Today we have some remarkable women who lead the way for all women to admire and emulate. Women such as Oprah Winfrey and Nancy Pelosi — these women are using their lives in ways unavailable, even unheard of, just forty years ago. But they do it with compassion, care, and a sense of self that is unmistakably female. They have staked their claim in an arena where they feel they can make a mark, and they are doing so as women.

Congratulations are in order here for them and many more. Their work is not only having a major impact on women and men, girls and boys, but is also expanding the view of a woman's "role" in the world. Importantly, they do this not by challenging or competing for a man's role, but by bringing to bear on issues of importance the unique attributes and characteristics of women.

They have achieved a high level of fame, desired or not, that holds them apart in many ways. Oprah is a force for such good in this world, but not many believe they could follow her path.

Yet we feel certain that for every Gertrude Bell in history, there were other less well-known women of similar passion, working tirelessly within their own communities to improve the lives of those around them. And today, for every Oprah, there are many other women, lesser known, but with similar passion and vision.

This book, then, is based on the thousands of women worldwide who also have a vision, who are using their talents and making their mark. We went in search of these women and found them effortlessly and in great abundance. We found women simply following their "inner vision" and impacting multitudes worldwide, with no fame or fanfare.

So we say congratulations to the women you are about to meet in this book. They have all made a leap based solely on their vision, their passion, and a desire to be a symbol of good, thus becoming a symbol for peace in this world. They followed a vision, and now people everywhere are better because of it. These women, and the thousands of others they represent, are truly transforming the planet. Today they live by new rules, their own, living successful lives on their terms, and creating a positive force all over the world.

But, there is yet another congratulation that belongs here. And that is to you the reader. The fact that you picked up this book means you have either just taken a step toward realizing your own dream or are already on your path and curious about others like you. You are also a woman of vision. This book is dedicated to all of you out there with a dream or a nugget of desire, and a strong will to follow it through. Imagine it! Create it! Then live it!

Our hope, our vision if you will, is to introduce you to others very much like you, but who have already made their vision a reality. We will demonstrate how alike you are and how you can follow their lead.


**Mystical and Practical**

Our hope is for this book to inspire you to take those first steps. But we don't want to simply encourage your unique vision. We have also designed this book to provide you with a blueprint of practical guidance for proceeding on your path. We can all dream of great things, but it's those pesky first steps that can seem daunting. And those are followed by another set in the middle of our path. Face it, Dorothy didn't find Oz on her own. She had the support of others along the way, and a great mentor, okay, a *good* witch, who showed her a yellow brick road!

The women you'll meet in these pages have all been where you are, and found those steps, plus a few twists and turns along the way. Their own advice and guidance can assist you in directing, then navigating your own plan to realize your vision. And we can only imagine the lives you will impact.

From their stories you'll see how simple the first steps can be. You'll learn how to focus your own vision and begin to bring it out in the world. You'll learn of some wonderful ways to get started, without a total life makeover. You'll hear of many obstacles you might think you'll encounter, yet learn how these women viewed and managed them.

We tried to weave the commonalities among the women we interviewed with examples from what they told us and what they are doing. We wanted to show how they approach what they do and live their lives, the thread that runs through them that connects us all together. We hope you will find inspiration as well as practicality; they go hand in hand. You begin with your commitment, by *feeling* the inspiration that compels you to say "I will." Next consider the practical implications of your dream, such as: Where does money come in? How do you start? Will you be committed full-time or part-time? Where do you find assistance/advice? Most importantly, we share with you some of the wisdom these women imparted to us.

At the back of the book, we introduce you to each woman so you can know her and her story. Feel free to flip back at any time and discover someone who intrigues you as you read; they are listed in alphabetical order.

Importantly, you'll meet some incredible women and be inspired by their stories and the gift they bring the world and, just as important, the gift they receive back.


## A New World Vision

As more and more women step up and pursue their vision, reaching out to people all over the world, an incredible change is occurring. You won't see it on television. No one is tracking it statistically. You will see it in the faces of so many afflicted worldwide as they are supported and uplifted. You'll hear it in their voices — and one day it will overwhelm the cynical views of the world so prevalent in our media today.

As more and more women assume new roles in their lives, fulfilling their vision, women everywhere will realize a need to reach out and change their community — locally or globally. As this expands and spills over the world, the world will be transformed.

*I've learned there is a huge power with one person who wants to do something. You go in spite of what happens, you keep your vision, and you keep moving. I think the world tries to tell us there is power in numbers, but there's also power in one.*

*~ Becky Douglas*

***Rising Star Outreach***

# Chapter One

## Epiphany: The Power of Change

*One seed can start a garden*
*One drop can start a sea*
*One doubt can start us hating*
*One dream can set us free!*
*~ Kathleen Smith*

Americans love drama, and many of us believe it takes a life-altering event, such as a death or illness, for someone to push all fears and resistance aside and change their lives. And this does occur, but just as often the catalyst is much more subtle. The impetus for women discovering their vision and, just as importantly discovering their passion, is often not for the reasons you think of most. We wanted to begin by addressing this concept of change as an epiphany — whether it occurs as a major shift or a simple "aha!" moment.

It can be as emotionally impacting as learning of the plight of another that simply resonates within. How many of us have been up late watching television and came across an infomercial, then were suddenly dialing the phone through our tears at the plight of children in some far-off land? Or watching a presentation on St. Jude's as Marlo Thomas introduces us to those incredible kids and their courage. Personally, we love her shows and have been supporters of the hospital ever since first watching one.

But, it can also be as soft and simple as hearing a phrase that resonates within you, or coming upon a breathtaking landscape and allowing your thoughts to drift there. Something speaks to you in these moments, some place deep inside, and you can't let it go.

The link between all of these simple moments and a life-altering event is the passion accompanying the experience. This causes a new awareness and compels you to follow or pursue a new vision of your life. It comes combined with a lingering trust that there is a reason you now have this desire within you, maybe even a burning desire. Don't ignore it. Start down that new direction, that new path. It's going to lead you somewhere wonderful and quite possibly provide solutions or support to others you might encounter along the way.

This unfolding comes in different ways to different people. For some it might be dramatic and catalytic in nature, propelling one into dealing with a specific challenge. For others it is a process of gradual revelation — one thought leading to another, one circumstance evolving into another, or one meeting leading to another — that gradually brings the vision to light.

If you can allow that unfolding to occur, it can take you to some wonderful places. This might run the gamut of experiences and emotions, from simple to complex, from interesting to cathartic.

What has happened in your life that has "thrown you for a loop"? What made you stop and reassess? Every woman, if open to it, can allow the experience of a catalytic event in her life to propel her into her vision. It is not the vision itself, by any means, but it is an event that so moves her, she is compelled to find out the significance of the event and translate it into purpose.

## The Event

Any event can cause a shift in our thinking, our focus, and alter our path, even one degree. But as a ship sailing the ocean, a one-degree course change will guide you to a totally new destination. For example, one night Sandra Clarke was starting her shift as a critical care nurse for Sacred Heart Medical Center in Eugene, Oregon. Her first patient was an elderly man who was near death. He asked her to sit with him, but her duties took her away for one and a half hours; by the time she returned to his room, he had died — alone. This affected Sandra so profoundly that it led her to eventually develop *No One Dies Alone*, a volunteer pastoral care program that provides companions for those near death who have no one else. The program

2

has since spread across the country.

Some women are moved into this new phase of their life through necessity — the responsibility of becoming the family's breadwinner or having to significantly add to the family's income. It might be through an illness — two of those interviewed were cancer survivors and both recognized it as a gift, for the opportunity it brought them. Two other women have always worked at jobs to support themselves, leaving their passions on the side, and later, in retirement, are thrilled to be able to now do the work that feeds and energizes them.

Sometimes an "aha" moment can be a catalyst that provides us a needed focus to alter our course. It could be as simple as coming upon a beautiful mountain view and having our breath halt. Victoria Hatch remembers her experience when she was in Idaho. "I was up in the mountains and I had some time. I was by myself — no kids with me, and I had time to just go and sit for a while." While there, she had an overwhelming sense of knowing that she was missing a huge part of herself and that she had been running away from who she really was. She felt she now needed to get back on track and "remember myself, remember who I really am." Victoria grew up in Minnesota; her grandfather was Native American, from the Widers reservation on the northern border. But her grandfather moved his family, including her mother, off the reservation early and wanted his family to have no part of it. He had been traumatized in his younger years by the schooling that the white world had forced upon him, devaluing his Indian heritage, and was determined "not to be Indian." He believed that living in the white world would make it easier for his children to mix in and adapt.

Victoria is of mixed blood and grew up walking in two worlds, white and Indian, but never felt like she belonged in either one of them. She decided it was easier to be white because the world around her was white, and it seemed to be easier to blend in.

But all that changed in Idaho, sitting in the mountains. It would lead Victoria first on a quest to find the huge, missing part of her life, her heritage. Then it would change her life again as she felt compelled to become a bridge between the two worlds, especially for native children. Her work today extends to conferences and seminars through her organization, *West Wind Seminars*.

For Kathy Headlee, a simple event occurred around 1990. Kathy had always raised her children to reach outside of themselves; she ensured they had ample opportunity growing up to give and serve and have an understanding of how other people went through life. But then came a fateful day in San Diego when she and her family were watching a video and were introduced to a crisis happening in orphanages, first in Romania, but ultimately around the world and, specifically, Africa. This touched her as nothing else had, the plight of these children and what they faced in life. Our very civilization could be impacted by this growing problem. This concern would alter the course of Kathy's life. She founded *Mothers Without Borders,* starting small, with Kathy organizing efforts to get volunteers to go and work in orphanages in Romania. Then it grew to multiple trips annually to several countries. Finally, in 2000, *Mothers Without Borders* was incorporated as a 501(c)3, an official nonprofit organization, and Kathy quit her job to manage it.

Monica Willard has always had a need to be involved and to connect to people who care about issues and the world. But with a husband who traveled extensively and small children at home, there was little room in her life, so she volunteered in community activities. This led her to the American Association of University Women, which would ultimately lead her to the United Nations. At a UN "Value Caucus" around 1986, she heard a speech given by Anwarul K. Chowdhury, former Under-Secretary-General and High Representative for the Least Developed Countries, Landlocked Developing Countries, and Small Island Developing States. His message was on the "Culture of Peace." It stuck with Monica, who would later tell him, "You gave me my life's mission."

From that day on, her vision became clear. Today Monica works diligently with the United Religions Initiative, a nonprofit organization within the United Nations. This initiative was formed in order to have dialogue that reduces religiously motivated violence and to create cultures of peace and justice for the earth and all living things.

The Reverend Carole O'Connell looks back, and instead of one catalyst, a series of progressive "directions" occurred, leading to her mission — playing out first through ministry, then as a life coach, author, and speaker. But in the mid 1970s, Carole didn't have a purpose or a mission in life. "I was just moving through life, lost in the weeds."

After leaving an unhappy life situation and marriage, Carole moved her children to Florida, where she would embark on an incredible journey, meeting people who led her in new directions. During her first week in Florida, a friend asked her to go to church, and although this was not a part of her life, she went to a New Thought service where "I fell in love, I fell passionately in love." She immediately resonated with the message and would realize later she had been "divinely guided" to pick up and leave everything behind and discover her path.

Carole would spend the next several years studying, taking courses, working with others along her path. She realized she wanted to teach people to be self-empowered. Carole gave herself a deadline of five years to study and create a life of spiritual work that would empower others.

She discovered ministerial work during this time and felt an incredible joy there. She was asked to create and give a Sunday service for a church in Florida, which scared the heck out of her, but it led to creating other services. One day after giving a service, a congregant asked her, "Why don't you be a minister?" Then it all clicked, something she had never considered. But she knew that was how she wanted to live out her vision.

After more than twenty-five years in ministry, culminating in building the largest Unity church in Atlanta, Carole realized this cycle was complete, but her vision was not. She now had a drive to work with people individually, yet also a dream to share her vision with greater numbers. She retired from the ministry in 2005 and went in search of her next role, whatever it would be, to achieve this.

That role, which is still evolving to her great joy, revealed itself to her as a writer with her first book, *The Power of Choice: 10 Steps to a Joyous Life,* in 2006. Her next book for children was published in 2008. She also currently dedicates much time to speaking engagements as well as individual life coaching. Her message of self-empowerment and the joy it brings to your life is being shared in greater and greater numbers.

## Catalytic Events

A catalytic event can absolutely drain you, make you want to hole up and escape the world. But it can also catapult you in a new direction if you allow it. Even the scariest of events, such as a diagnosis of cancer, can propel you to find the positive and move yourself to pursue a passion.

Annie Manes did just that after a diagnosis of breast cancer in November, 1989. In her early fifties at the time, she said, "I truly felt I wouldn't see another Thanksgiving, but I made a determined effort to find other things to put into my life, other than dwelling on cancer."

Annie had always directed her life with a pledge to be happy, and as it had in other trying times, this drive would support her now as well. That wasn't to say she didn't think about cancer every day for a long time, but she took classes and got involved in things that would release her from the chain of feeling so different because of the diagnosis.

These classes led her to an amazing group of new friends, with whom she would later start a writing group, suggesting they even write a book. "We gave ourselves six months of writing, with the thought of other people in mind," according to Annie, "of writing in ways that would be beneficial to someone going through our experience. I had sort of a feel for this, and as I did with most things in my life, I just went with my gut and whatever seemed right, and in pure intent, we worked into this book."

*Shades of Meaning: Four Friends Facing Cancer's Challenge* was published as a thank you to their oncologists, nurses, hospital staff, and others who had entered their lives during all their cancer experiences. But further, it would be a guide to others who faced the same events they had. It would become a comforting source within doctor's offices and libraries and could be found in local bookstores. "We left something tangible for people to pick up and look at; we turned a negative into a positive."

Kate Atwood lost her mother to breast cancer when she was twelve. In college, she decided to volunteer at a camp for bereaved children because she figured she was healed and it would look good on her resume. On the first night, she was asked to stand on stage and share her experience with three hundred strangers (something she had *never shared* with anyone). It became the most powerful, liberating moment of her life.

Later that same night, a little girl came up to her and asked if she could tell Kate her story. Kate listened as this girl told her matter-of-factly how both her parents had been killed in a car accident. Kate later found out that this girl had completely shut down but in that moment had had a major breakthrough. That night Kate made a vow to herself that no child should have to walk that grief journey alone. It gave Kate her "voice," set her on the path to true healing, and led her to her life's work, *Kate's Club,* which she now runs full-time in Atlanta.

One of the most dramatic stories we encountered in our quest for these women of vision came out of a heartbreaking tragedy here in the United States, but one that was to have a life-altering impact on thousands in India.

In 2000, Becky Douglas, stay-at-home mom of nine children, was faced with one of the hardest things she had ever done. Her eldest daughter Amber, diagnosed as bipolar eight years previously, had committed suicide. While arranging her funeral, Becky was going through her daughter's things and found that Amber had been sending money to India to sponsor an orphan. Becky and her husband made the decision to honor Amber by asking people to donate money to the orphanage in lieu of flowers.

People were so generous, and so much money was raised that Becky was contacted by the orphanage and asked to be on their Board of Directors. Before she made up her mind, she decided to travel to India and see the orphanage for herself. She found that the orphanage and the orphans, by India standards, were pretty well off.

However, on the streets between her hotel and the orphanage, she witnessed such suffering on the part of the leprosy beggars she encountered that it haunted her. On her return home, she couldn't sleep. Finally, she figured she could have insomnia for the rest of her life, or she could do something about it. That's when she decided to try to help one leper child to a better life. This one small decision set in motion the events that would take her all over the world and change many other lives.

Becky would ultimately meet Padma Venkataraman, the daughter

7

of India's past president, who had been working to build a unique way to make leper colonies self-sufficient, using micro lending. "We began working together to organize micro-lending groups, 'Women's Self-Help Groups,' in the colonies," stated Becky. This spiraled until these businesses were supporting the colony and getting the women out of the begging circuit. When Becky met Padma, there were ten colonies already operational, but the money had run out. Today, working together, these two women have now redirected the lives of those living in forty-five colonies and have received invitations all over India to open up their program.

Today Becky's *Rising Star Outreach* includes the micro-lending program, various businesses in forty-five colonies, mobile medical clinics, an extensive volunteer program, and a school where lower and upper caste children now learn together; and they are building homes for orphaned children.

Importantly, Becky knows that her daughter Amber's life was not in vain. "It was a very meaningful thing that happened with her. It was a catalyst for amazing accomplishments impacting the lives of so many Amber would have wanted to help. She would be happy, at last, to see it all." When the Marriott Foundation agreed to build two new children's homes for *Rising Star Outreach,* they notified Becky that one would be called "The Amber Douglas Home for Girls."


## Necessity of Change

Many catalysts come simply from our own needs, to support our aging parents, or a family member, or many times, our young children after a divorce. Barbara Stanny, best-selling author of several books, including *Prince Charming Isn't Coming: How Women Get Smart About Money,* was the daughter of the "R" in H & R Block. She had a lucrative trust fund and was raised not to concern herself with money. She had been taught that her husband would manage it. And he did. A compulsive gambler, he went through most of it, until one day Barbara went to the ATM and there was no money. She began to learn about money then, and now empowering other women about their money has become her focus in life.

Andrea Shelton's life spun on its axis when her older brother, through a strange and bizarre confluence of events, was sentenced to fifteen years in prison for a fender-bender at a stop sign. Although his sentence was later modified and he served only eighteen months, her mission in life became to serve those in prison. Her inspiration, taken from her brother and her faith-centered life, focused on a quote from the New Testament, Matthew 25: *I was sick and you visited me, I was hungry and you fed me, I was naked and you clothed me, I was in prison and you visited me.* Now through her *Heartbound Ministries*, she has over fifty-five thousand brothers and sisters in the Georgia prison system.

## Giving Back

Several women we talked to spoke of being directed to find ways to use their life experience and gifts to assist others. This can take many forms.

Wendy Daly had no idea why she was compelled to go on a church trip to Nicaragua. Once there, she observed women in the villages whose lives were very difficult — no cars, no electricity, no conveniences. "These were women who never went more than twenty miles from their village." She watched as they washed their clothes in the river by hitting them against the rocks. It seemed they had no way out of their poverty, their hardships. And then it hit her. *She* would be the way. But that was all that came to her at that point.

Wendy is a professional hairstylist and owner of two successful salon spas. She knew she could teach many of these women how to cut hair and in the process give them a portable way to make a living. She didn't have a plan then, and she fully admits that the impulse took her more than she took it. Today, she has founded *Indigo Sky,* a foundation that allows her, through her salons and with several of her staff, to reach these women in Central America, sponsoring them and personally instructing them how to use their own hair stylist skills to support themselves and their families.

Heidi Kuhn had been intellectually following Princess Diana's work involving the eradication of landmines, in the news in 1997. At the time there was a group on a nine-city tour speaking on the landmine issue, culminating in San Francisco the month after

9

Diana's death. Although Heidi had been taking time out of her career in TV journalism to raise her children, she also felt a strong need to stay involved in current events. She had been using her home to host various social and political events.

A representative for the tour asked if she could host a reception at her home for these speakers in a few days' time. Heidi had three kids and a new baby she was nursing, and the house was a mess, but she was compelled to immediately say yes. She then hung up and asked herself, "What did I just say?"

She threw the whole thing together in less than a week, winging it, and on that night really learned so much more about the landmine issue. She was so moved by the experience, she felt compelled to make a simple toast, "That the world may go from mines to vines," which was met with a profound and respectful silence. In that very moment the course of her life was changed. Today, *Roots of Peace* has removed landmines and planted vines in thousands of acres in Angola, Cambodia, Croatia, Bosnia, Iraq, Afghanistan, and the Kyrgyz Republic.

## Personal Epiphanies

Jan Dahlin Geiger began listening to tapes of Brian Tracy. She did not know then that this would lead her to create opportunities for people everywhere to learn to redirect their financial life. She had recently shifted her financial career from one with nice big paychecks to commission based in real estate investments and was listening to tapes to learn to refocus herself. But Brian Tracy was to introduce her to a simple concept that would impact her life, then and in the future. In Jan's own words, "He is phenomenal, and the thing that got me was the thing he said about setting goals." A Yale study conducted years earlier followed a graduating class. Three percent of this class had written down clear, specific goals; twenty years later that three percent earned more than the other ninety-seven percent all put together. (This study has since been updated at Harvard with similar results.)

These statistics caught Jan's attention. As suggested by Brian Tracy in his tapes, Jan began listing her goals for faith, family, friends, fitness, finance, fun, finishing touches (learning goals), and "for others." That was when it began for Jan — the "for others" part — the service and "giving" goals. When she wrote that down and began considering it, she realized she wanted to do something consistently, not random acts of kindness, but something that would consistently serve the greater community.

Today, years later, Jan has written a book designed to reach young people, especially those graduating college, about personal finance. *Get Your Assets in Gear!* instructs them on how to realize their life goals financially, and enjoy all their rewards. She took the basic ideas she learned at a young age and implemented over her lifetime, matched it with her incredible experience in the financial world, and passed this on to young people just starting out in life. Next, she began designing seminars to teach these same principles to reach anyone who was living with debt and lack; turning this all around in their own lives. *Get Your Assets In Gear Workshops* are held several times annually now and continue to be taught by Jan herself.

As a young child, Serena Woolrich was inspired by the work of Simon Wiesenthal. The daughter of a Holocaust survivor herself, she recognized the work he was doing to expose the Nazis and to help the survivors. She wanted to help the survivors, too. As she grew, she became involved in various groups, and then with the advent of the Internet, she saw a way to create a community in cyberspace where survivors, their children, and grandchildren could connect from all over the world. She could help many of them find specific answers to what happened to their relatives and get some semblance of closure. Serena's *Allgenerations* does this and more; these connections have become a resource for historians and documentary filmmakers.

## One Dream Can Set Us Free

These are just a few of the examples whereby women have found a way to empower themselves and impact pockets of people all over the world, giving them the tools and inspiration to make their own path. Their journeys took them to a variety of places, challenged their own concepts of themselves, and, without exception, gave them great joy.

Each had a catalytic moment, and each and every one of them stood at the brink of choice. Their lives could just have easily taken a different turn. It was their choice. They each made the decision to take one step forward. No one went from the recognition of the moment that defined her life to creating a huge organization the very next day. Each woman started with where she was at that particular moment in her life.

Perhaps you have an idea for something you want to do — and you haven't been able to articulate it. Perhaps you are wrestling with making sense of it. Perhaps you are in the sacred place of "I don't know."

Know that there's something inside of us when there's great intention. We do all have a deep purpose for being here. We say we want to know who we are — we want to be real, we want to serve — and yet, we want to *define* how all that's going to happen for us. It doesn't work that way. As Wendy Daly stated: "You really just have to go with it because it's really not that much about you." Learn to follow your interest.

**Some Suggestions:**

1.  Start by thinking about your experiences. What gets your attention? What are you drawn to or seems to reappear in your life? What have you seen or experienced that moved you or shifted your paradigm — your view of the world? How has it altered your perspective? Has it moved you into thinking something should be done? Have you given any thought to what you *could* do, what you would *want* to do if there were no obstacles or fear standing in your way?

2.  As suggested by Brian Tracy and used by Jan Dahlin Geiger: Think about the different areas in your life and write down your goals: Faith, Family, Friends, Fitness, Finances, Fun, Finishing Touches (Learning), and For Others. Review these areas of your life and give yourself a grade in each area based on where you are right now. Then see how you can expand in

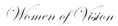

those areas that need a little bit more attention. That's where you just might begin to find your vision.

3.  Shift now to what could be your intention about these experiences. Can you begin to verbalize it based on what *you want*? That's where so many of the women began, and it took them places that were way beyond anything they initially dreamed. Some of these intentions were verbalized early on as:

I want to help one leper child to have a better life.
I want to bring people together.
I want to help the world go from mines to vines.
I want to help people find the joy in their lives.
I want to give people hope about their money.

Darlene Ballard, author of several books, including the inspirational *God's Rose,* which enlightens and supports those in prison, told us, "When I have an epiphany moment, an 'I finally get it' moment, I write it down. I write down the lesson that I've learned from it, and many times it eventually becomes a new book."

4.  The next step is just to talk about it. Put it out there. "You know, I'm thinking about _____. What do you think?" If you have a vision, or start to have one, you have to begin to communicate it, talk about it, and bring it out. The vision then starts to become a reality. Our suggestion in the very beginning, before you have really focused your vision or dream, is that you only talk to people of like mind. These may be family members, friends, associates, kids, clubs you belong to. You may be at a tender stage at this point, and if you know, based on past experience, that a particular friend or family member will not be supportive — that you will be shot down and shut down — do not discuss it with that person.

5.  Now start to expand on your vision. Put your idea in writing

and articulate what it is that you want to do. Bring it out of the "thought world" into the physical world. We can't recommend enough the power of journaling when you have ideas. It gives you an outlet to explore your thoughts and ideas as well as a history of how things evolved.

If you can take these first five suggestions, you will begin to move in the direction of what you want to accomplish. You will be well on your way to creating what you are beginning to dream.

# Chapter Two

# Beginning: Energize Your Inspiration

*...understand that whoever you are, you have something significant to offer the world and you can't quantify what it is.*
~ Kathy Headlee

W omen are visionaries, mystics, seers, prophets, *dreamers*. They see the world as it is and visualize how it can be, how it can *become*. At the beginning, one's personal vision may not be clear at all, but if you can take a step out in faith, take a risk, you can begin with yourself and ask: "What can I do to make a difference?"

## Divine Discontent

A lot of women say, "But I don't have a vision, I don't know what I want! I just want to do something, I want to feel meaningful, or I want to have a purpose. I just know I'm not happy where I'm at now." That feeling of discomfort is the biggest challenge for most women — and the place where they begin to think about what it is they *do* want.

But the truth is you don't have the capacity to know because you are too stuck in where you are right now. All you can think about is what is wrong, and there is nothing that can come to you at this point. So you must start with where you are and accept that may very well be the place of "I don't know." As Margot Swann, *Visions Anew,* says: "You don't know what you don't know, but it's out there." And "there" is in your mind and heart. You may even have a small inkling of what it should be.

## The Key Is To Put Yourself Out There

Try something. Put yourself out there — look into your business, in your community, in your church, or in your political arena and see what the need is. Barbara Duffy from North Fulton Community Charities told us: "There's so much need in the community in all kinds of different arenas. It can be political, it can be service, it can be business; it can be all sorts of things. Just open your eyes — something will grab you — but you've got to be looking."

And don't be afraid to choose the wrong path. Sometimes you find out more this way, like who you are and what you really want, either through mistakes or by becoming involved in what you think *may* be your passion. What you can discover is what you don't want, which can lead you to what you *do* want. It is all right if you find out what you have become involved in is not your passion, because dollars to donuts, along the way you *will* discover what that truly is. Jan Dahlin Geiger, *Get Your Assets in Gear!,* recommends: "Get into action, do something, anything, anything, anything. I really believe — ready, fire, aim. You can make course corrections later."

Just say yes! And you don't have to say yes to something huge. You can start out small. You can do something in little ways because that allows you to make changes as needed, including finding that this direction is just not right. Once you begin to do something, other opportunities for interaction and information become available to you. For example, a student who has always dreamed of going to law school goes to work in a law office and finds out it is not what she thought and hates it. But because of contacts and information she has garnered *at* the law office, she discovers social work and finds her passion.

As Reverend Nancy Worth, Unity North Atlanta, says: "It's kind of like the Energizer Bunny. He goes until he hits something, but then immediately turns and goes in another direction." It's okay if the first thing doesn't work out. It may not be what you thought, but there is another message for you within that experience. Or, you may find your passion right off the bat because you put yourself out there and became involved in a particular topic or program, and now you are pursuing it — no matter on what level or what time frame in your life.

So start to think about all the things in your life that you *get* to do and move in that direction of enhancing, expanding those things. If you don't take a step and try something, you won't start down any path, and if you don't start down a path, you won't be going anywhere, and it will be difficult to find your purpose.

For every person who lives by an excuse that they cannot do something, there are those who will jump in and do it. They find fun and joy in the doing, a path opens, the money comes, and their lives are changed forever. You have to decide which one you want to become. Whatever it is you choose, it should energize you; it should make you feel delighted to get out of bed in the morning.

Once you have discovered whatever it is that brings you that sense of purpose, that joy, it is more important to follow the intent of your passion than worry about specific goals in creating whatever form that passion takes at the beginning of your journey. *Allow* it to come to you. It was clear to us that we met amusement on many different levels when we talked about specific goal setting — at the beginning. At the beginning, the women we interviewed did not worry that they were or were not achieving specific goals. They just had the passion and excitement to get started and wanted to do it immediately.

## Start Where You Are

It can be overwhelming to start a project, an organization, or service. But remember, you don't have to start something new. It is possible to begin to create your vision right smack dab in the middle of what you are doing and where you are right now. For many women, their passion is found in their current job or in their family. Their dream is created *within that paradigm.* For example, Stephanie Nelson, The Coupon Mom™, left the corporate world after ten years to stay at home with her children. Her first realization was that "If I want to keep this job of being a stay-at-home mom, I better get smart and learn how to save money." That was her first impetus for finding a way to make a science of saving money at the grocery store and cutting her food budget through the use of coupons.

To sit with a dream or a vision and see the end product can feel wonderful, and then appear quite overwhelming. Getting from here to there seems quite a long journey. But if you travel anywhere at night, you realize that although you can't see the end of your journey, you learn what route to follow, then simply follow the small amount of space in front of your headlights. You can only see a few feet ahead of you at a time, but you know you will eventually arrive at your destination. And you can travel all the way from Seattle to Miami that way.

Laura White got an idea for *Wild and Water,* her initiative that provides swimming lessons for low-income children, and was able to start it under the auspices of an already established nonprofit. She had no resources, and they were willing to include her ideas in their program. That way she was able to test it out and see how it would work before she launched her own initiative.

You can take the same strategy to follow your dream, your vision. As Tricia Molloy, *Working With Wisdom,* states: "That whole concept of setting an intention, an affirmation, but not getting caught up in the details, that is so critical." Don't get caught up in the details or what the outcome will be like. Do what you can do today.

Becky Douglas used to ask herself, "What can I do? I'm just a mom." But after turning the tragedy of her daughter's suicide into the catalyst for building a major organization that supports thousands of women, men, and children in countless ways, she no longer asks that. However, eight years ago she started with the vision of helping one child with leprosy to a better life and moved in *that* direction, one step at a time.

Once she knew she could do that, she trusted the details and direction would come along. So she started with no idea where it would lead. She got an old slideshow projector and took pictures she had taken in India and turned them into slides. She then invited twenty people into her home and showed the slides. "I told them I was going to start a charity and see if I can't go over and help three people." That evening all twenty signed up to sponsor a child. She thought then, "I can find twenty kids from the colonies' homes." Then one of the people present at that first meeting asked her to come speak to her church, and someone else offered their civic club. This spread by word of mouth, and *Rising Star Outreach* was born.

She was raising the money, but now did not know how best to use it in India. Suddenly, the woman who would become her partner, Padma Venkataraman, called out of the blue. "She never mentioned she was the daughter of the former president of India or that she was very famous in India. She had the most wonderful organization in India set up to help those in need by helping themselves. She had a vision, too. But she had just run out of money." She said to Becky, "Let's partner." This was a theme that was to happen again and again to *Rising Star Outreach* as they changed lives for thousands in India. In Becky's own words, "I think that God really cares about the people in the world, and when He finds someone willing to do something, He helps them."

Together they now help thousands of women, children, and men in India support themselves, which has gotten them out of begging, providing a way to help support their colonies. Becky herself now speaks in front of groups as large as five thousand as well as at national conventions.

Margot Swann was a full-time mother and stepmother. Her life was absorbed into the life of her rising attorney husband. His ambitions were her ambitions. She did everything to support him and the marriage. Then, one day he informed her that he wanted a divorce. Her world changed completely, but it eventually brought her to find her passion.

Choosing to take the high road at every opportunity with her husband during their divorce led to a lengthy process — three years — but she looked at it as a gift, allowing her to process everything she had to go through. During that time she sought out support and information. She had to find counseling, financial planning, an attorney, and a new career — in order to begin a new life. She began to think of that journey that every divorced woman takes, and eventually she founded *Visions Anew*, which offers programs, support, and resources for women who are divorcing.

*Visions Anew* did not come to her all at once. Margot had been a Spanish major in college and had no idea what she was going to do in the work world. She started out by developing her own travel agency, and the passion and purpose she found there was in talking with people who wanted to vacation or honeymoon. She would draw from them the type of experience they wanted to have. Then, she would match them with a great travel location and experience. As the travel business started to change, she began to look around for something more meaningful to her. Through a sequence of events, based on her own experience and her work experience, she formulated *Visions Anew*, which actually does the same thing for divorcing women — determines what they need, what kind of experience they would like to have, and then helps to match them up with attorneys, financial planners, therapists, career counselors — a path to their new life.

Today she impacts the lives of thousands of people through her website, her retreats, the support groups her organization sponsors, and the talk show she has on a local radio station. She is continually expanding her network of resources, all with the goal of helping women who are now taking the journey she herself experienced.

Stephanie Nelson became an expert at saving money. When the local food pantry had a food drive, she read the list of needed items, and it struck her that they were all coupon items. She thought it would be fun to see how much food she could buy with coupons — which turned out to be fifteen dollars for sixty dollars worth of food — and donated it all to a local food pantry.

But as she was sitting in the waiting room of the food pantry, Stephanie was so struck by the number of people in need, she *knew* she had to do something. She started a simple website to list the items — to teach and encourage others to cut coupons and feed the hungry. Then one day she got an email from a person who had visited her website: "My family has saved so much money since we started using your website that not only are we saving money and making ends meet for the first time, but we were able to donate to our own church's food drive this year like everyone else." The "like everyone else" struck a chord within her very being. She asked herself, "What does it feel like not to be able to give when everyone else is giving?"

It became her mission to teach others to save and give through their saving. Today she is known as the "Coupon Mom," and Stephanie's free website has grown, to over four hundred thousand users, and offers a wide variety and range of ways to save and to give. She has been on *Good Morning America* seventeen times and is now partnering with major newspapers across the country to get the message and saving techniques out to the public. It has provided the opportunity for her to make a difference with her life as well as financial security for her family.

Kate Atwood learned early on that kids, especially in bereavement, need to have honored their ability to build relationships with those who make them feel comfortable and safe. So she began to think about ways to create a comfortable and safe zone for kids who had lost a parent or a sibling.

From this desire, *Kate's Club* was born. It began with a few thousand dollars that Kate charged on her Visa card, and not a clue about how to find these kids or where to take them. Her mission today is to empower children and teens facing life after the death of a parent or sibling. "We're about building a community of hope and of healing and of fun."

There is a Quaker saying: "Let your life speak." What does that mean to you? What are the ideas that come to you when you envision your life speaking to others, your legacy? What is the story you want to tell about your life? Would you prefer to cry because it's over, or smile because it happened?

**Some Suggestions**

1.  Start with yourself — what do you *like* to do? What do you know? Then look around in the community and see who needs you and your skills and what you like to do. Laura White, *Wild and Water,* puts it this simply: "I would say that if all of us took what we really love to do — whether it was playing soccer, or knitting, or baking cakes — take what you love to do, and see who is in need in your community." She suggests www.handson.org as a great place to start. "See what agencies are around who need activities and bring what you can do to them; they will really appreciate it, and you'll appreciate it at the same time. You'll be sharing your passion with someone else who wouldn't be able to enjoy it otherwise." Your passion may be raising dogs, fishing,

shopping, creating a home, sewing, children, or even money. Those skills are needed in your community on a variety of levels. Start somewhere and see where it leads you.

2. Spend time every single day in meditation or in silence, listening. Where are you being sent to next? What are you being told to do? If you will listen, then when you get the little nudging, follow it. We hear "Go with the flow" all the time. But what if you did? What if you just listened, then when you *felt* you should do something, just did it?

3. We suggest you set an intention before your meditation or time alone. Speak what you want, state your goal, voice an affirmation — whatever you want to call it. But always add to the end, "This or something better." Then allow yourself to follow your inspiration.

Every single one of us can do *something*. That thing can come from your experience, your skills, your interest, your heart. Breathe deeply and ask yourself that question: What can I do to make a difference? Know that you are not here just to take up space on planet Earth, but to live a life of significance for yourself and those around you who breathe the same air you do. You would not have picked up this book if you didn't *feel* that. That is the true beginning.

# *Chapter Three*

# FEAR: THE MYTH OF LIMITATION

*You have to take risks in life or nothing good is going to happen to you. I have a friend who says when I'm about to take a risk, I consider the downside. If it's not death, I do it!*
~ Chellie Campbell

Once you have articulated intention, the biggest challenge you may face is resistance to that intention. It seems the moment we decide what we want, we have the experience of thinking of all the reasons why we *can't* do it. Chellie Campbell, in her wonderful book *The Wealthy Spirit: Daily Affirmations for Financial Stress Reduction,* refers to these as "Yeah, buts" and advises you to take those words out of your vocabulary.

Be aware of resistance. Claim it and know that it is just part of the process you will go through. Understand that challenges and obstacles appear in any endeavor you will ever attempt, just as they occur now, at all times of your life, no matter what path you follow. They are always there in our lives; it's not the obstacle that impedes us, but how we view it and ultimately, what we do with it. Your attitude will be the key to overcoming any challenge along your path.

Learn this truth and make it an intrinsic part of your very core. An obstacle is really a challenge for you; it is *always* an opportunity for something. The only time an obstacle will stop you is when you do nothing. If you do anything to work with or around it, anything at all, it will always create an opportunity. View it this way and you'll understand why many people believe that obstacles are the gift of possibilities in their lives.

## The Sum of All Is Fear

There are as many forms of resistance as there are individual women. So many of the women we talked to started out by asking themselves, *But what can I do? I am just one person. How can I afford to do this? I am a single parent — how can I juggle home, work, and what I want to do? I am too old; I am too young — none of my friends are doing anything like this. I am just a mom; I never had a job. There is no time with my career. Where will the support come from?*

Okay, let's name this right now. The obstacle behind all these and others is really fear. And yet fear is not an obstacle at all. It doesn't really exist. It's in our head; it's not tangible. It's not age; it's the fear that we're too old or too young. It's not that we don't have time; we fear spending our time on this new endeavor — what will happen to our lives as we now know them? We fear a loss of security; that people will laugh at us, won't understand us — we fear change.

But, you're reading this book, which means this is probably what you most want right now, change in some area of your life. And fear is really what is behind your immobility. Yet, what we fear never really occurs. It's more an exercise our mind generates as we contemplate stepping out of our normal way of doing things, our normal day-to-day lives. So what might possibly be our ally in this internal battle? Again, it's all in your head.

## Your Own Personal Superheroes

Passion and commitment. One fuels the other. The more passion the better. Passion is the strongest level of feelings and the one that can kick any fear out of your head — or at least place it somewhere on the sidelines. Problems, obstacles, "naysayers" — you will probably encounter them all. But if you are truly committed to your vision, instead of viewing these as bad things along the way, you'll see them for what they are. They're simply a guide for you to help gauge your direction.

When we hear no, we want to stop. Take the advice from Wendy

Daly, *Indigo Sky,* to get to a place where you simply do not take no for an answer. In her own words: "If you have that passion in your heart, you need to make that decision that you are going to do it. And then don't be discouraged if the door shuts; it's a guide, it's not a no. It's a guide to where you should be going. It means this is not the door to go through, so go find another door. Don't give up your passion, go to the next door."

Wendy further cautions against ever taking these negative responses personally. "It's like McDonald's. If you ask: 'Hey, do you want fries with that?' and the answer is no, does it hurt your feelings? No, they just don't want fries. So go find someone who does. Keep going and find someone else."

Our women of vision encountered a myriad of obstacles starting out along their paths, but found that their passion and belief in what they were doing led to a perseverance and refusal to give up. It would inevitably lead to incredible flukes, or chance occurrences, coincidences, or what we many times call just good luck. The truth is if you move continually forward, regardless of how small the steps, you will encounter that luck. You'll meet like-minded people to work with; others who want to support your efforts; doors that suddenly open.

Kate Atwood of *Kate's Club* started out part-time, after work, by developing outings for kids who had lost a parent or a sibling. This was originally to be a once-a-month event. She had a small fund-raiser at a sports bar and immediately raised about $2,000. She had a connection who gave her box seats for the circus. Everything was in place.

Her one teensy problem: she didn't have any kids. The week before the event, she still hadn't found any parents who were willing to turn over their child for an afternoon. What parent was going to hand his or her kid to an unknown entity at this particularly vulnerable moment in the child's life? None of us believes that we live in Mister Roger's neighborhood anymore.

Kate solved this problem by making an important connection at a children's hospital and putting together a presentation for several parents (including references, a resume, business plan, etc.) and then arranging individual meetings. It turned out this was overkill. The first parent put the presentation aside and asked Kate to tell her own story of losing her mother. It was Kate's *own experience* that gave her credibility and dissolved her perceived resistance. Today *Kate's Club* is a full-time job for Kate and reaches out to hundreds of children every year to ease their pain after losing a family member.

Carolyn Miller is a photographer who is moved to create pictures that reflect the beauty and goodness in the world, even though every day we are confronted with things that are not so good. Upon retiring from her job, she was able to devote much more time to her photography.

Inspired by the movie *Pay It Forward,* she began to think about how we are all connected, how we are all bridges, one to another — bridges of humanity. Then a chance conversation occurred. Carolyn had a friend who ran a theater, and Carolyn jokingly asked her: "One day when I grow up, will you let me have an exhibit at your theater?" Her friend promptly replied: "You're already grown up. When do you want to do it?"

Now Carolyn immediately hit another form of resistance we all know well: panic. The thing she wanted most was right in front of her, and she was overwhelmed with what she wanted to present, not just a picture. She wanted something that visually appealed to all the senses of the audience in terms of telling a story, touching them in some way, so that when they walked away they could honestly say they learned something from what they saw. She hadn't a clue how to do it. That overwhelmed her almost to the point of immobilization…until she realized it wasn't about her. It was about the subjects she photographed.

Through immersing herself into that reality, focusing on those she had photographed and their stories, Carolyn was able to release the resistance, and the rest was very easy. Her first exhibit was a great success.

The key is to look at these challenges as opportunities to reassess or to discover ways of tweaking — or making shifts, whatever that might be — in order to accomplish the greater intention. If you have that vision in your head, you need to make the decision that you are going to do it, no matter what.

Your commitment will help you view challenges as a wonderful guide. For our women of vision, it transformed their lives, gave them direction, and introduced them to people, places, and events they wouldn't have known existed otherwise. They all feel so strongly about what they do and what they have become, and now it is as natural to them as breathing air. But that was not so in the beginning. They all encountered challenges, large and small. But their commitment kept them focused and, more importantly, active, which in turn transformed any obstacle into a guide to move them forward. Passion fueled their commitment. And this would limit all their fear.

So, what were some of the big challenges these women faced? We bet they're some of the ones you're experiencing yourself. But not for long.

## The Myth of Age

Mark Twain once remarked, "Age is an issue of mind over matter. If you don't mind, it doesn't matter." Amusingly, a couple of the women we interviewed had at one time viewed it as an impediment, but from both sides — as being too old to start something new, and too young to be taken seriously. Our youngest woman of vision was seventeen, and our oldest was in her late seventies.

Laura White, seventeen years old and founder of *Wild and Water* and coordinator for *Dream Prom Project*, told us that a big challenge was her age. "Sometimes I find that because I'm a kid, people don't take me as seriously as I'd like, right off the bat." However, once she gives her presentation and explains what she is about and what her organization has already accomplished, it gets so much easier. Then she notices the exact opposite; people get more excited *because* she is so young.

On each end of that spectrum they recognized the challenges of age — but ultimately used it to their advantage instead of their disadvantage. Their commitment and their passion for what they wanted, and well-rehearsed words to describe their focus, ultimately overcame any issues of their age.

A lot of people believe that it's too late for them, that they're too old to start something totally new. They could have accomplished great things when they were younger, but now, no; too tired, too poor, not enough energy, etc., ad nauseum. The truth is you are not too old, and it's not too late. You just might be a second-half player. While we are not a fan of sports analogies (hate them), this one works. How many times have we heard of a game where the players on one team were well behind the other, only to come back after the half and blow the others off the field, or court?

Perhaps *you* are a second-half player. If so, you are in good company. Julia Child was almost fifty when she published *Mastering the Art of French Cooking* and then became a television legend. Emily Post was in her late fifties when she wrote her classic book on etiquette. Grandma Moses was seventy-six when she first turned to painting. Mother Teresa was forty when she launched the Missionaries of Charity as an official religious community, and Ann Meara wrote her first off-Broadway play in her mid-sixties. As Barbara Sher says in her book, *It's Only Too Late If You Don't Start Now*:

*If you can stop wanting what you were taught to want and start searching for your own goals, if you can stop fearing failure and start to see it as nothing but an institution of higher learning, you will find something amazing: Right now, right here, in the middle of your life, you are poised to do something extraordinary based on who you really are."*

## The Myth of Time

Janine Bolon faced a much different challenge. Janine is founder of *SmartCents, Inc.* and author of *Money...It's Not Just For Rich People!* and other books. Her vision is to spread the essential principles of wealth accumulation and financial independence to all, to change views on money, and teach new habits for financial independence. She began by teaching the principles she herself had not only learned, but also lived. However, she realized that it all hinged on her. She couldn't reach the numbers she wanted all on her own, especially as she was also a wife and mother of four. It took too much time from her family. When asked about her greatest obstacle, she replied, "Me. I am my own worst enemy. That is my biggest obstacle; there is not enough of me to go around. I can't split me up."

But Janine had had the good fortune to meet the late Sam Walton when she was in her teens, and she remembered his great advice about running your own company: *Learn to replicate yourself.* So she decided to find a way to do that. During a recent interview Janine told us, "Everybody was telling me that the model you want to use is the mastermind type where you train people to replicate you and do it, but that's not going to work for me. What I have to do is get people financially independent, so unless I want to coach someone for ten years, depending on how much debt they have, that's not going to work. So the only way I have been able to replicate myself has been through books and audio products. This is the only way I know to replicate myself at this time." And she continues today to look for another, new model to replicate herself, ensuring she continues to be financially independent, supports the widest possible audience with her highly successful methods, and, foremost, continues her primary role as "mom" to her kids.

Desiree Scales encountered a similar obstacle on her fast track-career with Delta Airlines. Originally a flight attendant, Desiree had moved into Corporate Communications in 1996, and the next year Delta needed to join the burgeoning new electronic movement and launch an intranet. Desiree was drafted and was educated in the software and what little other education existed at the time, and she joined the ranks of the early pioneers in this developing communications field.

Later, after her first daughter was born, Desiree felt a similar resistance to working full-time at a corporate headquarters. She wanted to provide her children all the attention she could. She approached Delta to allow her to work from home, but this concept was still a few years ahead of its time; she was turned down. After a meeting with her husband, mother, and sister in-law, in which they all wholeheartedly supported the idea of launching a web design business, Bella Web Design was born. It would grow over the next ten years to one of the most successful web design companies, serving over three hundred clients in thirty-five states and earning the #1 ranking from kudzu.com.

Over the years Desiree began to see a growing concern in the electronic media forum — firms and people misled and often harmed financially due to a lack of knowledge of this quickly expanding industry. From this, Desiree would launch her personal vision to educate people and businesses to stop fearing the computer and take a more active role in their online personality. A way to give back for all her success, she now speaks and educates people on the Internet, its uses, and how to make educated decisions on their needs and uses of web-based media, something she calls a consumer's "bill of rights" in the cyber world. All this from a challenge of how to remain a fiscally viable part of her family and still be the mom she wanted to be.

## The Myth of Skill

Many of us feel almost trapped by life — we can't do what we really would like due to time and job constraints. You get paid, a little or sometimes a lot of money, to do what you're not happy doing. Maybe you don't feel your job is fulfilling you at all. Could this be you? A recent article referred to these people as the *Working Wounded*, stating seventy-six percent of employees in this country say they do not like their job!

The truth is it doesn't matter what you do in life — how much you are paid for it, or if you are paid at all. There are avenues for you. And you'll find you probably have all the knowledge and experience you need to follow your vision now, or if you take stock of your life, you'll see you are developing the skills and experience you will need.

One of the chief patterns that developed from the study of these women was that most had many different "careers" before they got to where they are right now and found their bliss. They benefited from all the learning that took place in each position. In all their work, different skills and talents were developed that came into significant use in the new path of passion that was now unfolding for each woman.

So, think about your journey, the different jobs you've had, the different skills you have obtained. They have all led you to where you are right now. Think of them all in terms of how they can be used in making your vision, your dream, a reality. Take the best, that which you enjoy the most. Focus on it. Could you, like Kate Atwood or Laura White, begin by doing this part-time? Or could you possibly even volunteer in a similar arena?

Or, you might need to learn other skills, or about other cultures, or even a new language. Volunteering is such a great way to do this and could require as little as one day a month. With access to the Internet comes a variety of ways to do that and plenty of organizations to help. Two good places to start would be www.idealist.org and www.volunteermatch.org.

You could also join associations in the area of your interest. You might need to become a public speaker in order to get your message to more people or to raise funds for your idea. You might be a natural at this, or the very thought of getting up in front of a group of people and speaking in coherent sentences might give you nightmares. Public speaking is a skill. While it is true that some people are better at it than others, the bottom line is that it is a skill, and it can be learned and developed. A great association to learn and practice this would be the local Toastmasters organization in your area.

Almost any skill area you require will have an association dedicated to teaching it and supporting those interested in learning. "Google" what you want using a search box technique. Type in the subject of your interest and add ": associations." For example, if you wanted to find Toastmasters or similar organizations, type "public speaking: associations" in the search box.

## More Than Joshua's Mother

Hopefully, these few examples will give you the idea that it doesn't matter who you are or what skills you have. If you have an idea, you can begin to build it. And you can start today. Tomorrow will take care of itself, with or without your conscious direction. You're creating your life tomorrow with every act you take today. How committed are you to making your dream your reality?

These women would not have created any of their amazing organizations or services if, when they felt they were limited in what they could do, they had simply accepted that and left it there. No, they went beyond the barriers they had set up for themselves of being just a mom, or just a businesswoman, or lacking a formal education or experience. Intuitively they knew they had to have something that was completely of their own making that fulfilled a need and ultimately gave them a purpose they could love.

As Barbara Duffy, North Fulton Community Charities, says: "You've got to say okay, I'm more than Joshua's mother. Being Joshua's mother is a wonderful thing, but there is life beyond. I need to find something that makes me, gives me as much fulfillment and pleasure as raising a kid until they are twenty-one or whatever."

### Feel the Fear, But Do It Anyway

So start now, right where you are, and remember:

- Limitation is a myth. You determine what you can and cannot do.
- What do you feel when you think about what you'd like to do? It should take you up the scale of positive emotion. It might even give you goose bumps.
- List the best of what you've done, those things that made you the happiest, the things you liked doing the most. What skills did you acquire from these? Are there any you still wish to obtain? What resources could you find, including volunteering, that would provide this experience?
- Feel the passion and you'll lose the fear.

Importantly, remember, your best opportunities could be the obstacles you are now encountering. Look beyond them and you'll find your possibilities.

# *Chapter Four*

## Passion: Not Just For Prophets

*If you have something stirring up in you — that's what's guiding you — that is your soul trying to connect you with spirit. You have got to take that leap; you have got to follow that inner voice in order to fulfill your purpose.*
~ Laina Maxwell

Prophets are visionaries who believe their direction comes from a spiritual source and feel passionately about imparting it. And passion is, without a doubt, the most powerful experience for all women of vision. As Reverend Carole O'Connell, *The Power of Choice: Ten Steps to a Joyous Life,* puts it: "Probably the most important thing was I found my passion. When you find your passion in life, you're unstoppable. Finding my passion, I found my joy, which is what life is all about." Each woman we spoke with feels so strongly about what she does and what she has become because of that passion. And most realize that their passion was ultimately what fueled their commitment to their ideal, their vision, allowing them to not only launch, but continue to thrive against any obstacles. They no longer give it any thought; they have *become* their passion.

The Spanish playwright Lope De Vega stated it best when he said all you need to do theater is a "platform and a passion." This is simply that overwhelming feeling about an initiative combined with your commitment and added to your vision. It is the same for our women of vision — in order to fulfill that deep desire within, they each feel that passion and create a platform on which to express it. Over and over we heard that the most important element was the discovery of individual passion. Once a woman of vision finds her passion, it empowers her, makes her feel like she can do anything. It energizes her; it gets her up in the morning and keeps her going all day. It brings her joy. Over and over we were told that it was that individual sense of passion about their purpose that fueled our women of vision and gave them the energy to meet the challenges and opportunities of each day.

## Feel Your Passion, Change Your Life

But the true benefit of passion is that it is personally transformational. And it usually comes with a belief so strong that it is visceral. As Heidi Kuhn puts it: "I believed in my heart that seventy million landmines silently planted in seventy countries is wrong. If we remove one landmine and plant one grapevine, it is an action for peace on earth. It is a tangible action." Once this idea took hold and she felt the passion behind it, obstacles, objections, and fears became secondary, and she was able to work her way through them. From this Heidi grew *Roots of Peace*.

Barbara Duffy was raised with a strong sense of community service that propelled her life forward even though her husband's career demanded they move eleven times in sixteen years. Each time, she would find a place where she could become involved in the community surrounding her new home. Barbara started out in all these communities volunteering. She has been involved in all facets of running an organization, the recruitment of volunteers, fundraising, grant writing, dealing with people in crisis. She learned her strengths and weaknesses and over time learned to focus on what she did best. That in turn made her feel better about herself and what she was doing — a win-win situation all the way around.

Later when she needed to find employment, she was able to transition her volunteer work into paid work. She had all the skills necessary and knew the organization. Now she spends her time getting paid for what she loves to do, supporting her community through North Fulton Community Charities.

## Passion Fuels Commitment

Sandra Clarke knows all about commitment. A critical care nurse, her passion to develop a program within her own hospital became a fifteen-year journey. She had a vision for a program to support those dying alone, inspired by Mother Teresa's comments upon receiving the Nobel Peace Prize, where she stressed that one should always die in view of a loving face. Beginning in 1986, Sandra continued to discuss her idea with fellow healthcare professionals and administrators, and although everyone thought it was worthwhile, no one knew how to execute such a plan, and it went nowhere. But she never gave up. In 2000, she once again found herself explaining her concept at a three-day ethics conference. A nearby pastoral care director overheard her and asked her to write a proposal, which he later took to the corporate office, and within one year, *No One Dies Alone* was born. Today over nine hundred hospitals have requested a guide for how to implement the program in their area.

Pat King has always been convinced, even as a little girl, that the world is a place of infinite possibility. She maintains that we come into the world with a blueprint, but what we build from that blueprint in our lives is entirely up to us. As part and parcel of that fundamental belief, she is convinced that everyone has a calling, a purpose, a talent, and the responsibility to share their gifts with others. Her blueprint is the execution of her passion and purpose — spreading truth through love and greater awareness. She lives her dream by creating an environment for people to discover that power within themselves. Her work is transformational, and she teaches individuals to deepen and go inside to find that blueprint. She guides them to the discovery of exactly what that is for them so they can enhance it with their own particular choices. She does this through seminars and retreats and works all over the country with people of various ages and both sexes.

Carolyn Miller enjoyed developing her love of photography for years, but continued her career with Bellsouth. Her retirement from work would later afford her the opportunity to combine her passion for photography with her vision of exploring the bridges between people. She wanted to present the incredible beauty and goodness of people she found who daily confront the challenges of this world, but without accolades — people she feels are truly altruistic.

Marnie Pehrson's passion for her own writing career and commitment to helping others discover their purpose led her to the creation of *IdeaMarketers*. This online platform is a vehicle whereby other writers can enhance their visibility through the delivery of their message using Marnie's comprehensive, powerful, and effective promotion program. It affords them the opportunity to reach tens of thousands of potential clients, and allows Marnie to nurture developing talent. Today, she is evolving that into a coaching and seminar program as well.

These few examples should show you that it doesn't matter who you are or what skills you have. If you have an idea, you can begin to build it. And you can start today. Let tomorrow take care of itself. One of our favorite quotes has to do with commitment. How committed are you to your dream?

> *Until one is committed there is hesitancy, the chance to draw back, always ineffectiveness. Concerning all acts of initiative (and creation) there is one elementary truth, the ignorance of which kills countless ideas and splendid plans: that the moment one definitely commits oneself, then Providence moves too. All sorts of things occur to help one that would never otherwise have occurred. A whole stream of events issues from the decision, raising in one's favor all manner of unforeseen incidents and meetings and material assistance, which no man could have dreamt would have come his way. I have learned a deep respect for one of Goethe's couplets*: "Whatever you can do, or dream you can, begin it. Boldness has genius, power and magic in it."
>
> W.H. Murray, *The Scottish Himalayan Expedition*
> (J.M. Dent & Sons Ltd., 1951)

## Feeding Your Spirit

Before we interviewed even one woman, we decided to leave the issue of religion or spirituality out of the mix. We were concerned there might be a sense of discomfort among readers that one had to be grounded in some form of religion in order to be a woman of vision. However, every woman insisted there was a spiritual component with her vision, and expressed it in a variety of ways. It was an overwhelming pattern, certainly the strongest by far we encountered in our search. As Marnie Pehrson, *IdeaMarketers,* so clearly articulated: "A lot of this has been a spiritual journey for me. The major pivotal points were spiritual awakenings, or reaching a higher level spiritually."

Each woman, in her own way, and using her own definition, referred to how guided she felt by a higher source, spirit, or God — the wellspring of inspiration. However, *all* were adamant that their sense of passion was absolutely and completely interwoven with their individual belief system. And the women we interviewed were from a myriad of religious and spiritual backgrounds — running the gamut from Jewish to "Hindu Christian" to New Thought — ranging from conservative to liberal. Each one looked at herself as an instrument, at times moving forward, kicking and screaming about the task she knew she had to accomplish, but with a deep knowing sense of her purpose and resulting joy in the unfolding of that process. As Barbara Stanny, *Prince Charming Isn't Coming: How Women Get Smart About Money,* so aptly put it: "Nothing in the world happens that is not spiritual."

Each woman came out of her individual experience and, without exception, now thanks a higher source for it because it has brought her to where she is right now, and that place is one of joy, of living "on purpose," of feeling passion for what she does every day. Each woman's journey was different, but they all ended up at the same destination — the development of passion for life and purpose, grounded in belief. Chellie Campbell, *Financial Stress Reduction Workshops,* said it best: "I think the people who are getting ahead, especially for women, have the strongest connection with God or Spirit, and you know, a sense that this life isn't all there is. It may be all that is, we can't prove it, but I don't want to live this life as though that were the case. It doesn't work for me; that belief just doesn't work for me." Andrea Shelton, *Heartbound Ministries,* simply put it this way: "I think God puts a vision in everybody."

## A Place to Find Your Passion

Pat King, *Transformational Ministries,* believes you may be living two lives. You may be living the human paradigm that everyone else does — meaning the labels we've created that we think are true, such as those built around economics, relationships; all these labels that we have — mother, wife, friend, breadwinner, caregiver. The other life is in a place of greater truth, which is built around whom you really are, and the need to follow your authentic path. You may be at the point where you feel discomfort in the balance between these two lives. Perhaps you need to stop trying to mix both lives together and ask on the deepest level: "Who am I?"

She suggests a journey to empty, empty, empty. When you don't have that conflict going on within you, your "guidance" may come by just saying, What's next? How can I serve? You've now reached the point of saying "Yes!" The guidance is so true and strong on what is next that you just go "Yes!" There is no questioning now if you have the passion to follow your vision. But you do need to empty the labels and the paradigms that do not line up with your truth.

## Are You a Bridge Builder?

Over and over, the image of bridge builders — even the very words — appeared in the interviews. Victoria Hatch feels her mission is to build a bridge between the Indian and white worlds. Of both white and Native American heritage herself, she learned that she had to heal that dichotomy within herself first. In that process she was told by the Elders she spoke with that: "You have an important mission to do — you are supposed to be a bridge. Because you belong to both of these worlds, you are to learn how to bridge the two worlds — how to build bridges of understanding." Through that learning process evolved her *West Wind Seminars,* where she helps Native kids with the same questions; they come to understand and appreciate the power of who they *truly* are.

Kathy Headlee recognizes the needs of a hundred and forty-seven million orphans in the world — an exploding segment of the world's population who are being raised without adult care and supervision. She also sees that in this same world another population is exploding — those in the developed countries who have huge amounts, by world standards, of discretionary income, time, and talent. Through *Mothers Without Borders* she tries to create a bridge that could bring these two groups together. This allows both groups to feel joy; one is provided the necessary resources to improve their lives, and the other is provided a new sense of fulfillment.

Kathy is the first person to tell you that the needs of these orphans are beyond overwhelming. But, she figured out how to execute her passion by doing it one step at a time. The first time she went to Romania, she wanted to ship supplies — medicine, clothes, etc. She was told it couldn't be done, but she just broke it down and figured it out, and now her organization ships about forty tons of relief supplies each year. She didn't start out doing that, but that is what she does now, stepping out in the faith that she *could* do it. She says: "Follow your heart and just know all you can do is take one step at a time. You don't have to create something huge in one day."

Marnie Pehrson sees herself as a bridge builder as well. In fact, her favorite poem is one entitled *The Bridge Builder* by Will Allen Dromgoole (see poem at end of book), and for her it's all about the things that she has figured out in her life. She doesn't feel she can rest until she eases the burden for the next person passing this way — imparting her knowledge.

Carolyn Miller developed a photographic exhibit she entitled *Bridges of Humanity*. She talks about how we are all connected and that people really are making a difference and moving the world into a place of higher awareness — doing it one step at a time. "In that process they are creating bridges — those are the paths on which other people will walk."

In our research, we found that this is an apt description of what every woman of vision does. If you are considering what moves you, think about yourself as a bridge builder. How can you be the catalyst that connects what you feel strongly about with the world around you? It may be in your own family, or in the wider community of your neighborhood, your town, or even the world outside of all that. How can you build a bridge?

## Move in the Direction of Your Dream

Life is not static, it is dynamic. Many people discover their passion at a point when they need or can make a change in their lives. Their vision is so strong they want it to take up the greater part of their lives, and devote their time and work to this. The women we met who fit this scenario made changes through their lives in their work, but stayed true to their vision. Reverend Carole O'Connell is a woman whose passion never changed, but the expression of that passion changed over the years. She has accomplished many different roles throughout her life as minister, writer, coach, and seminar leader, but her passion for what she does centers her life and burns as brightly as ever in all her endeavors.

When you put the energy of your passion into the world, it comes back to you in many ways, through ideas and projects that occur to you, pushing your dream forward, but also through those you inspire with your enthusiasm. As you get excited about your initiative, energy will be returned to you in an abundance of ideas and suggestions for moving it forward.

Ask yourself: What do I really feel like doing right now? Then go and do whatever answers that question for you — take that *inspired* action. As you continue to do this and trust that this is the most appropriate action for you to take, you will discover that you easily find solutions to whatever challenges you have and will continue to move in the direction of expanding your vision.

Focus on the big picture of your dream, but continually ask yourself: Am I moving in the direction of what I am asking for? Only you can decide how to approach your dream. But focus your vision with your passion behind it, and it will continue to speak to you, no matter what. Once you have a vision, it will not go away. And you can trust, or have faith, that one opportunity after another will present itself.

Tune into the voice that speaks to you. As Laina Maxwell, *The Power of Awareness,* puts it: "It's through that tension — that burning desire to do something that's real — follow that. That voice is your music, that is your calling. For some people it may keep them going for a year, and that leads to something else that leads to something else — but always listen to that voice. Don't die with your

music still in you. "

**Some Suggestions**

1. Reverend Carole O'Connell counsels her clients to use a "Contrast Chart" to bring their desires into focus. She graciously allowed us to provide it to you here. Take a sheet of paper and make two columns. Under the left column write out something you are unhappy with in your life; write it as a sentence, not a one-word description (work, relationship, kids). Next, write some detailed sentences of what is not right about that area beneath that line. Then flip it. In the right column take each sentence and rewrite it as if that area *were* working in your life. Write what that sentence would read if things were joyful in that area. Do this for each sentence. Now delete or erase the left side. Read what is left. This is a great indicator of what you do want now. This is a great exercise to give you some guidance for what you really want to create. For more on this and other exercises visit: www.caroleoconnell.com for links to Carole's book and other resources.

Look over the Contrast Chart. Are you getting an idea of what your passion is?

2. Start by developing your "elevator speech" or, if you live in California, your "Hollywood pitch." This requires no expertise — just write out the end product or service you see in your vision. Make it as clear as you can see it. Then turn it into a quick, thirty-second paragraph, or about sixty to seventy words. Read it *constantly*. Recite it to yourself, your spouse, kids, your best friend. Know it and feel it. Then use it to tell people what it is you want to do. Be prepared to also say what obstacle you might currently be facing, because more often than not, their response will be "That's incredible. What is holding you back?" or "Where are you in the process?" And there is nothing wrong with an honest "I don't know where to start." In this way, you will be guided to those

who can help you, who will ask you: "How can I help?"

When you are passionate about something, things start to happen very rapidly. That excitement draws to you new opportunities and solutions you might not have thought of otherwise. Passion creates such a strong energy that it can literally run right through obstacles that appear in your path, and show you ways around any blocks you may encounter.

Whether you are a prophet, create a nonprofit, or operate for profit, recognize that more and more women are beginning to find and know their passion through their own guidance system. You have one. Learn to listen to it.

# *Chapter Five*

## Trust: Jump and The Net Will Appear

*The place of 'I don't know' — that is the most powerful place to be. You have to trust that it will come to you, that you're making a transition, you're moving forward, it is going to be gradual. I don't ever suggest you just jump off the mountain, that you just quit your job cold because you are unhappy — but allow it to unfold.*
~ Reverend Carole O'Connell

One of the themes that stood out during all of our interviews was the importance of trust in your life. Time and again, every woman we talked with discussed this, and several made this the essence of their advice because it was trust that set them free to pursue their vision, and they believe that it is trust that will set you free to pursue yours as well.

It's not too far a leap to understand how important this would be to anyone embarking on expanding their life, enhancing it to enrich their world and elevate their own joy. It seems a leap of faith is part of any path not originally taken. At some point all women of vision had to trust their vision, their process, their God or faith, or trust their purpose. Without trust the rest really cannot unfold, and setbacks can be viewed as major obstacles. Without trust, doubters and "naysayers" are given too much credence, flippant remarks are granted importance, and molehills become mountains.

Every woman we talked to discovered that along the way, she could trust that once she had found her vision and learned to focus on it, the road opened up, the support came, and the resources that were needed appeared. But she had to have faith and trust that it would do so. And you have to trust as well.

<br>

*Kathleen Smith & Elizabeth Ireland*

## Trust the "Woman's" Intuition

We heard this over and over again. Listen for and then trust that still small voice inside yourself that guides you. Listen to it and you will get that little nudging to follow a certain direction. Then do it, follow it. It may take you in directions you never expected and certainly may not have originally occurred to you. No one ever mentioned a straight line to what they wanted to achieve. It took them on many twists and turns, but because the women relied on their intuition, it always brought them to people, places, things, *funding* they would not have found otherwise.

Andrea Shelton, of *Heartbound Ministries,* gave us what had to be one of the most incredible examples of this trust in action. Andrea, a lawyer by trade and now stay-at-home mom, had recently made it her mission to have the chaplains in the Georgia prison system reinstated. Her brother had been unfortunately, and as it turned out, wrongfully imprisoned. In attempting to connect her brother with a prison chaplain, she learned from the head chaplain at the Department of Corrections that the state legislature was about to cut the line item for prison chaplains out of the budget. Regardless of spiritual focus, most of us can understand how this act of budget cutting could affect many lives that really need support and direction.

Andrea tried many different paths to get this politically reviewed, all to little avail. A devout woman, Andrea couldn't give up and finally broke down in her shower, crying and asking God for direction. She knew her faith would produce an answer. She just didn't count on it happening so quickly. Fifteen minutes after she got out of the shower, a stranger from Macon, Georgia, who had heard of her concern for the prison chaplains, contacted her. She told her she must talk directly to the governor, and then told her to go that day to his offices and look for a particular woman by the name of Joy. "Tell this woman your story," she instructed.

That is exactly what Andrea did, even though her mind was saying, "How in the world am I going to speak to the governor?" She doubted she could get an appointment with him, but right behind that came the thought: "I can do this." So she went down there and simply said: "I need to meet with the governor." They put her in a waiting area where Andrea believed "they put those they think are crazy. What are we going to do with her?" But they left her sitting there.

Then, a woman named Joy came in to use the telephone to call her dentist. Andrea knew now what was happening in her life. She walked up to Joy and told her she really needed to talk to her. Joy listened to her story and told her she might have to wait all day, but she promised she would get Andrea an audience with the governor. And she did. And he agreed to help Andrea.

Stephanie Nelson had a similar experience. Almost three years into her *Cut Out Hunger* program, she was finding she had to do thirty hours of data entry to update her website each week. She got an idea to approach four companies and ask each for $5,000 in sponsorship money a year. That way she could hire a person to do the data entry and use her time elsewhere. But at that time she didn't have enough traffic on her website, and her idea was rejected. It became more and more difficult for her to keep up with what she wanted to do, and she was struggling. So, one night she decided to pray — not to ask for the money but to take away the drive, the obsession with the $20,000, and be satisfied with what was given to her.

The next day she decided not to turn on her computer. Then she got a phone call from a PR agency wanting to know how her website had become the entire focus that day on the radio talk show of a well-known consumer advocate. She didn't know. That same week Georgia Tech called her and told her they had decided to take on a project that she had proposed to them months ago, and would build the software for her website — software that she still uses today — which allowed her to expand nationally. After that she appeared on *Good Day Atlanta*, then *Good Morning America*. Today she makes much more than the $20,000 she was so insistent she had to have, and does not rely on any of the four companies she initially approached. There is also a *Cut Out Hunger* Scholarship Endowment at Georgia Tech that goes to a student who has done something to help feed the hungry.

Trust is a simple concept if you have faith. This could be as grand as faith in being a co-creator with a greater source, whether you call this God, Goddess, or a universal source or intelligence. Or you could simply trust that persistence does always produce results.

What's important is that you believe it and stay focused on it. Never believe that pure luck is a factor on your path, but know that your passion will provide you all the resources needed to direct you and sustain your vision.


**Focus on the Vision**

Our women of vision also counsel to avoid getting caught up in the details. Focus on your vision, your dream, and trust that it will unfold the way it should. But not always in the way you expect.

Tricia Molloy, author of *Divine Wisdom at Work* and the upcoming *Take Your Higher Self to Work,* tells her clients to trust that if they are inspired to do something, they have what it takes to do it. "You're not given an idea without the resources to accomplish it. So trust that you will be guided, from a spiritual perspective; you will find that you will be attracting people and resources that will be there to support you."

Tricia knows that most of us live with a need to control, but it is really an illusion of control. She has learned to relax into "All is well, it will all work out. I just need to do my part, and the rest will fall into place." And she learned that what she imagined to be true or what she was trying to do many times would take a different form, but ultimately her vision would be achieved.

Your job should be to place your focus on your vision and take baby steps daily toward it, but don't get caught up in trying to control all the details. There is a hit song of the same title from the *Rolling Stones* that speaks to this; in the chorus Mick Jagger sings, "You can't always get what you want, but if you try some time, you might find, you get what you need." Who knew Mick was such a sage? But it is correct. Do not focus on controlling all the outcomes — focus on the vision. See it, feel it, let it keep you inspired, and support your dream. Then take actions consistently, but let faith or the universe or intuition or your small voice, whatever you want to call it, guide you.

Reverend Nancy Worth has learned this through her circuitous road to her vision. Her early adult years had been spent on the stage in New York, and later in newspaper publishing, then as co-owner, with her husband, Bill, of a paper in Maui. And it was in Maui she encountered Wayne Dyer and felt the first great stirrings that there was something more for her life. She convinced herself at this point that her passion was for peace, especially after attending a program for peace in Russia in December of 1986, a trip organized by Wayne Dyer. The trip proved both thrilling and transforming as she met with peace committees and interacted with the Russian people, and Nancy became passionate about peace.

This set her on what she thought would be her path. But that route had a few more turns on the way to discovering her true passion. First she realized that although she had many talents and much experience to do almost anything, she could hardly create peace in the global outer world when people did not have peace in their own communities and she did not have peace in her own life. She knew she had to find a way to achieve this first.

Her own minister sent her on a path toward a spiritual education, which she began pursuing through an educational certificate program at Unity Institute in Kansas City. She threw herself into it wholeheartedly, but then another turn appeared. Six months into the educational program, she ended up applying for and being accepted into the Unity ministerial program.

Today she realizes her real passion was about empowering people, to reach them with a powerful message "that we don't have to be victims or cynics. We can step into our magnificence. We truly are the change we will see in the world."

She dreams now of reaching people through filling her sanctuary every Sunday, then to reach many others through her writing. She would like to combine her passion with her love of speaking in front of large groups. Ultimately she knows she will be speaking in front of thousands of people, directly through her ministry, and indirectly through other electronic forums. Nothing along her path was wasted. Her stage presence is now mixing with her vision to produce empowered and enlightened individuals, and ultimately that will bring about great change, and peace, in our world.

Nancy suggests, from her own experience, that you will know when it is right, when you are in the flow, because the doors will start to open. "I would know it was not a right move for me because the door did not open. Whenever something became a big struggle, I knew it was not the right path to follow." It's a simple concept, but not always easy. According to Nancy, "It shouldn't be difficult. If it is, you should seek another way. Don't give up your vision, just the task you might be trying to beat into completion." In other words, keep the vision, lose the need for total control, and learn to read the signs. If it is easy, then follow that path. If it is increasingly hard, then look for a new direction.

## Godwinks

Tricia Molloy expands on this wonderfully. She says you'll know you're in the right direction when you start noticing all the "coincidences" occurring around your vision. She calls them "Godwinks," inspired by the book *When GOD Winks: How the Power of Coincidence Guides Your Life*. These are those wonderful instances when you are focusing on your vision, or a piece of it, and someone or something enters your path with just what you need at just the right moment to move it forward. We encountered these constantly during the making of this book. We would meet someone and tell them what we were doing, and they would instantly get it and tell us, "You should interview this person" or "Have you considered doing this?" It was always incredibly useful information and proved to be the primary method for finding the women we highlight in this book. It also confirmed for us that we were definitely on our right path.

Heidi Kuhn, *Roots of Peace,* told us: "My grandmother would always tell me something that is etched in my heart: *Coincidence is a miracle in which God prefers to remain anonymous.* I see it daily. I just see these moments of convergence, and there is no accident."

We like both of these concepts. The point is that as you focus on your vision and begin taking your small steps, including the simple step of telling others about it, you will notice that ideas, people, and information start appearing in your life to help you with your vision.

Wendy Daly, owner of w daly salon spas, discovered this all along her path. She always had a driving passion to take care of women — a drive that came from a very painful and abusive childhood, which she knew had to have occurred for a reason. She became a hair stylist by trade and opened her first salon for women, but not just for hair styling. Wendy wanted women to have an experience, provide them a soft place to land.

Her intention was for all of her stylists and staff to be "Daymakers" every day, a concept she learned through attending a conference with David Wagner, author of *Life as a Daymaker: How to Change the World by Simply Making Someone's Day*. Their touch could be powerful, and the total experience, beginning the moment someone entered the salon, would make great days for their clients and make the company powerful and impactful. This would ultimately evolve into using her salons and stylists to improve the lives of some very needy women in Central America.

Wendy and her husband were out looking for a small church, something more personal where they could worship and feel a part of a community. The first day they attended St. Gabriel's Catholic Church, there happened to be a trip announced to Nicaragua, and *coincidentally* it was occurring on the exact dates she and her husband had chosen for a vacation.

Wendy had a feeling this was more than just a coincidence, so she and her husband signed up. That trip would ultimately lead to her creating her foundation, *Indigo Sky*, and years of supporting and working with women in small villages in Nicaragua to share both her knowledge and skills. Wendy knew she could help them improve their lives. "They had no outlet, no way out of poverty; they and their children were trapped."

Now Wendy and her stylists donate their time in Central America, and her salons sponsor women in cosmetology school, providing them a trade to support themselves and their villages. Recently, *Indigo Sky* expanded to work with targeted middle school girls in Atlanta, to better prepare them for high school. *Indigo Sky* is Wendy's vision, her slogan to help women "Live Your Imagination." According to Wendy it was "birthed out of people finding their own dreams through our company and the foundation."

Wendy's advice is if you have passion in your heart, you need to make the decision that you are going to follow it. And then trust that a route will appear. It may not be the exact way you imagine, or maybe you really have no idea of what route you should follow. That's okay. Trust that it will appear.

Laina Maxwell, *The Center for Awareness*, enjoys telling how one of her own sisters was inspired to follow her passion and how it all came together in one of Laina's workshops. Laina's sister, Leila Barbara, had always had a passion for interior design. According to Laina, "On the weekend she would do some things with it, but she would never leave her steady, corporate job. But several years ago, she was helping her neighbor, a good friend who is also quadriplegic, decorate her home. She wanted something pretty, even though she couldn't do it herself; she wanted something pretty to live in, so Leila helped her."

After attending her sister's workshop on *The Power of Awareness,* it all clicked for Leila, and she realized she wanted to live her passion and use it to help people with disabilities decorate their space. She left her corporate job and opened *The Orchidstrators*, in her own words "created to bring the same high-end decor and organization that we all enjoy and love to people with disabilities." She started that company in a leap of faith, and recently told her sister, "I now get what you meant by 'Life is fun and easy!'" (If you would like to check out Leila Barbara's amazing story and her company, visit www.theorchidstrators.com.)

But originally, listening to her fears, all she heard was you need security, you must have a steady job. She knew what she loved to do and had a dream. She told other people and spent some of her free time developing her craft, her love. The opportunity to help her neighbor started her thinking of how her talent could be useful. Then, another opportunity appeared when she heard about her sister's workshops. She just decided to attend one and see what happened. From there it all began happening for her, and she decided to take the leap. "Leila quit her job when she got back (from the workshop), she jumped into this business of hers, and now it's moving forward. It's so exciting." All these opportunities led Leila on her path to where she is today, and she tells her sister it's the best thing she has ever done.

Only you can decide how to approach your dream. Should it become your primary role in life, or will you mesh it into your personal or professional role as mother, wife, doctor, or any other avatar you relish? It can be as great or as simple as you want to make it. But it won't be ignored, trust in that. Once you have a vision, it will not go away. Focus your vision with your passion behind it, and it will continue to speak to you, no matter what. And you can trust that one opportunity after another will present itself to both guide you and provide you everything you need to bring it into reality.

The guidance will always be there. But we have this belief learned since youth to try to do things ourselves, try to have total control over all we do. It's embedded in our need to make our lives secure. So we try to do just that, attempt to control all aspects of our lives.

We try to "do our own thing." Yet, when we encounter resistance or obstacles, we might give up, use them as an excuse. How many times has this happened to all of us? We set goals and try to beat them into our life. Then, when it doesn't happen just the way we wanted, we decide it wasn't right and quit.

But you need to clear your ego out of the way, modify your old ways, and then just listen and try to live from total surrender. Get your head out of it. Merge into that space or void by saying, "I don't know what's next or necessary for me, but I can't wait to find out." Listen and follow what you hear, no matter how small or trivial it might seem. It always turns out better than you can imagine.

## Trust Yourself

Trust is a recurring theme. In all cases, you must trust yourself. Believe that when you need to know something, when you need to have something, it will appear. If you have said "yes" to your passion, you are trusting that what will happen may be the right thing or the wrong thing, but *something* will happen. It may not come in the form that you expect, so you have to become aware of and sensitive to what "walks" into your life or becomes part of your experience. As Pat King, *Transformational Ministries,* put it so beautifully: "I really believe that there isn't a place on my path that wasn't just absolutely perfect for what I needed to realize and to know so that I could do my work later on."

Trust is such a major factor in redesigning or even simply evolving your life to fit with your dream or vision. If you have the vision and it's clear, and you have the passion to support it, trust is the missing component that will clear the way for you to recognize

51

the help and support that will guide you toward your dream and change your world.

## Some Suggestions:

1. Several of the women we spoke with suggested keeping a daily journal. Each evening write in it, without fail. Include what occurred on that day, no matter how small, that aligned with your vision. Someone you met, something you found online, a coincidental event in your daily life, or maybe simply a thought that popped into your head. Write them all down.

2. Go back each week and review them. See how you might use them now to pursue your dream. You'll start to see patterns emerge, especially those that might not have occurred to you before. Follow those and see where they take you. Write this down in your journal as well.

Over time you'll start to notice frequent opportunities to further your dream easily. And you'll start to accept them quickly for what they are and follow their lead. Each time you will get more and more excited and energized, realizing that your vision, your dream, is really becoming a part of your reality.

You need only to focus on your vision, your dream. Then learn to look for all the opportunities, the coincidences, the "Godwinks" that will start appearing in your path. Trust that they will appear, then follow them and enjoy the journey.

# *Chapter Six*
## Guidance: Mentor, Guru, Or A Really Good Book

*My grandfather would just say: "Okay, Trish, let's just
sit here until you know what the gift is and what you learn
from it; then we can make an imprint on your spirit, and
then we can go out and have ice cream and go from there."*
~ Pat King

Most of us can look back on our lives and name women and
men who have had a profound impact upon us. This might
have taken many different forms — mentors, role models, teachers,
inspirational friends and acquaintances or situations, even workshops
and books — that inspired us and guided us. They were written or
conducted by people who sought to do just that. No matter who you
are, or what your situation is, there are sources of help and support
for you personally, professionally, and spiritually, to direct you along
your path.

## Mentor

In Greek mythology, Mentor was Odysseus' trusted counselor,
under whose guise the goddess Athena became the guardian and
teacher of Odysseus' son, Telemachus. A mentor is someone who
takes an interest in *you* and what you are doing. A mentor challenges
you to reach your full potential. She will guide you and help you to
grow. This guidance comes from without, but only makes sense, is
really useful, when it is internalized. Mentoring is the teaching that

goes beyond what you learn in school. It's creating an environment for you to grow. It sets the groundwork for your strength, direction, purpose, and ability. It can make a significant contribution to what you do and who you become. Your mentor's goal is to see you shine.

But this tutelage comes with a caveat. You only learn as much as you allow yourself to learn. You only receive the guidance that you allow to happen. And sometimes you have to *ask* for it. One of the women we spoke with is often asked for advice and guidance, but only gives it to those (about twenty percent) who keep pestering her. The rest she shrugs off, and if they take that first rejection as fact, she figures they weren't all that serious. So overall, it's up to *you* to let the mentor in. You must recognize the gift.

Most of the women we talked with, but certainly not all, had a mentor. Often, these mentors were part of their nuclear family — a person who took a specific interest in them. They encouraged and challenged them and helped to mold who they became. Often their mentors were a mother, an aunt, or a grandparent.

Barbara Duffy recalls that her mother functioned as a very strong mentor for her, particularly in the example she set. She remembers her mother doing many of the things she later did herself, including running the PTA. She never questioned whether or not she would be out working in the community, because that is what her mother did — through whatever organization she could find. It was not until later in her life that she learned her mother actually sat down and read books while Barbara was at school! She thought that you were always supposed to be doing something, and it became a permanent fixture in her life. As Barbara says: "I can't watch television without having needlework at my side — or something. I have to feel like I'm producing; otherwise I'm wasting time!"

Annie Manes, *Shades of Meaning: Four Friends Facing Cancer's Challenge,* fondly remembers her aunt Viv, who stepped in to raise her and her brother after her mother died in the 1940s. "Annie, you can do anything. Big girl, smart girl, good girl, she puffed me up and fluffed me up and made me feel, gosh, I can do anything!" Aunt Viv was also one of a small minority at the time to survive colon cancer, which would come back to support Annie later on in life when she was faced with breast cancer. Annie partly contributes her drive to meet all the challenges of her life to Aunt

Viv, including the decision to produce a support book for cancer victims while in recovery from her own personal cancer challenge.

Pat King's first mentor was her grandfather. Her mother left her with him when she was only three years old, and so for her formative years, she stuck like glue to him and learned many things under his tutelage. "For me, and you know it's different for each and every person, when I landed on this planet, and I really do believe we come in with a spiritual blueprint about what this life is for us and for me, I came in, even as a small child, with this incredible excitement about what a beautiful, loving planet this is." Her grandfather encouraged that excitement, and it has stayed with her for her whole life.

Mentors may come at all times, and may provide guidance and support throughout your life or be transitional, showing up in moments when you need them the most. Wendy Daly, *Indigo Sky*, has had several along the way. She remembers her first as Miss Ilsa, a woman who lived on her street when she was quite young. Wendy survived an abusive father and childhood, but when things got very bad, she would escape to Miss Ilsa's. There she would hear stories of Miss Ilsa's travels with her husband and about her life as a teacher and an artist. For Wendy, this gave her a picture of normality; these were kind people who treated each other with love. Wendy focused on that and learned how to survive her childhood.

Later on, Wendy began to see that people appeared as her life evolved and later as her vision for supporting other women by sharing her experience and skills came to fruition. This included an aunt who provided a refuge for Wendy and the opportunity to continue her education after she left home at fifteen; friends she met who guided her in her career and later provided financial support; and those who encouraged her as she developed her vision of assisting women and middle school girls.

She particularly credits Deborah and Edwin Neal — a couple who listened to her, gave her tools to work with, and connected her with a therapist when she didn't even know therapy existed. They believed in her and gave her a lot of opportunity. She still appreciates the generosity they showed to her and says: "They challenged you to reach your potential, and they cared more about this than whether you liked them or not."

Wendy also believes her children have functioned as her

teachers. When her daughter, Sage, was in second grade, she met an African-American girl in her class. This little girl wanted to look like a white girl, telling Sage, "I wish I had blue eyes, and I wish my skin was white, and I wish I had long blond hair." Sage just looked at her and said: "You can be anything you want except somebody else."

In some cases the person or persons who mentored our women of vision became *like* family to them. They found someone who they worked for in their career who really took the time to work with and challenge them. For example, Stephanie Nelson developed a friendship with Barbara Duffy, Director of the Fulton County Community Charities, and Barbara then became a mentor to Stephanie.

Mentors can come in strange and unusual ways. Pat King's second mentor was a woman whose name came to her in a dream! She asked everyone she knew if they had ever heard the name Pat dreamed of, as she was compelled to see if the woman was real or not. Eventually, she did find that the woman existed, and Pat called her and went to see her. It turned out the woman had recently lost her daughter, named Pat, to cancer. So when she got there, the woman said: "Oh! And since your name is Pat, you can give me a gift, because I sure do miss my daughter." She took Pat under her wing, and Pat credits her with having a huge influence on her life. However, the way she found her was rather unique.

Sometimes a mentor will just show up. Many of the women we interviewed discussed how people just show up when they start something new. Marnie Pehrson tells us that every time there's a major shift, there's a person who follows it into her life. "The first one was Alanna Webb, and she taught me the World Wide Web. Then there was my coach Jeannette, who was huge in my spiritual awakening, then Leslie Householder, who taught me the Laws of Abundant Living, which is a lot of what I teach — other people come to teach me as I need it." Marnie can now recognize the next pivotal person in her life by how her path is evolving. Her editor, Julie, came along when she was beginning her fiction writing, and now that she is evolving into speaking engagements, her speaking coach just "appeared" in her life.

Becky Douglas, *Rising Star Outreach,* received a phone call one day. Padma Venkataraman called her from India and suggested that they partner. All Becky could say was: *Who are you?* It wasn't until later that Becky found out that Padma had been at the United Nations for the past twenty years as the permanent Women's Representative, or that she was the daughter of a former president of India, or that Padma was treated something like a rock star in her country because of the work she does in the leper colonies and with micro-lending. They have been partners and friends since then, but Becky has also learned so much from Padma and freely admits how much she has influenced her life. In 2007, a PBS special was produced by Daryn Kagan about their friendship and their work entitled: *Breaking the Curse*.

## The Written Word

There were those who had no personal mentor — but when they needed something, found other sources. Many of the women we talked to cited the importance of books or workshops. A great way to find what you need, to move forward from wherever you are in building your passion, is to attend workshops or simply find the books on the subject. There probably isn't one subject in the world that someone hasn't written a book about. Sometimes you can find guidance through people who have built a reputation and a following through their seminars, tapes, and books. For Jan Dahlin Geiger, that person is Brian Tracy. She has been reading his books and listening to his tapes for many years. She credits him with really guiding her through her career. When she wrote her book, *Get Your Assets In Gear!*, Brian Tracy wrote an endorsement for the back cover.

For Tricia Molloy, this experience has been intuitive. An avid reader, she feels that most of the guidance she received has come from the many books she has sought out to find the information she needs. Her experience has brought her what she needed from the outside world as well, and she felt the minister at her church was a tremendous mentor both in terms of her message and the way in which she lived her life. She was also the best speaker Tricia had ever heard, and Tricia knew she wanted to be like her.

Laina Maxwell became addicted to books and workshops for over two years while evolving her dream to create her own seminar platform. She read just about everything she could get her hands on regarding her interests before she began to put her life's work together. She took a number of seminars, but it was the *concepts* that she encountered in them that inspired her vision.

She never did find an actual mentor, but found many ideas through the classes and the books she read. She even contacted some of the writers for more information. By the time she launched her business, she had read over two hundred books, taken a number of seminars, and done a lot of journaling. She was able to synthesize and internalize all of that and create her own system, *The Power of Awareness.* She has taught her weekend seminar many times and admits she learns something new each time she does it. And now she offers coaching, seminars, and support systems for others to discover the power within themselves.

## Make Your Own Support

You can also get creative and make your own network, as Tricia Molloy did when she was just starting her first business, a marketing communications agency. "I knew I needed support and guidance, so I started a group with four other women in 1989. It's grown to about a dozen women, and we still meet monthly to share ideas." If you are looking for support in your vision, most likely others might be as well. Create your own group to provide support for you and share it with others.

Try to meet in person — so much more comes out of these get-togethers than pure information. Mentors or support groups can provide wonderful links to others knowledgeable and useful in your path, but also provide uplifting moments of support when you most need it. Sharing our feelings is every bit as important as the information — we are women, after all.

Create your own "Advisory Council." Make a list of a small group of people whose advice you trust and ask them to help you formulate and articulate what it is you want to do. Desiree Scales did just that when she started her business, Bella Web Design, ten years ago. Her group consisted of her husband, her mother, her sister-in-law, and a friend. She gathered them around her kitchen table, and she laid out what she was thinking of doing. They all brainstormed, and their final comment was: "You're going to do great; you're just going to do great." Desiree appreciated their confidence in her, and she couldn't help but feel it herself. She knew from that moment, there was no turning back.

We did this as well during the writing of this book. Several of those we interviewed, as well as a few friends, agreed to be our advisory group. They helped us choose the title, edit the chapters, and even assisted with ideas for publishing and promotion. This kind of support is so helpful. So, you see, you don't really need to know all aspects of the new vision you're creating. You will find that others will provide the expertise you lack, and vice versa.

## Don't Forget Associations

A great way to find support and resources is to check out if any associations exist in the area in which you are seeking. Many do — and don't worry if they are not in your own location; almost all accept members from anywhere and can at least provide information and resources to you through online newsletters, chat rooms, or inquiries. These are great resources for articles, reports, grants, and other support resources you might use as you build your vision and launch your dream. Although almost all associations charge a fee, if necessary to your situation, ask about scholarships. Many do offer them to provide free membership or great discounts. Or you could volunteer for local events in exchange for free membership.

## Look for Role Models

Role models seem to hold an entirely different place in the lives of the women we interviewed. These were people they learned from, but did not necessarily know personally or have the opportunity to know really well. Several times Oprah Winfrey's name was mentioned as a role model — not because of her fame, but she is seen as someone who started from nothing and has been very true to what she stands for and uses her platform to expand upon that.

In addition to mentors, many of the women saw their mothers as role models. Kate Atwood's mother died when she was twelve, but she remembers her vividly: "She was a teacher, so she truly was about bringing out the best in kids. She worked with a lot of outreach children. She was one of those people who walked through life always trying to see the opportunities in it. She was a fifth grade teacher, and she had breast cancer in the early eighties. It wasn't what it is today. She had a bald head and, going through chemo and radiation, refused to wear a wig — it was too hot. Tried a scarf, didn't like that. She would walk into a fifth grade classroom bald. That was her opportunity to teach people about it. That was her opportunity to take some of the most judgmental, vulnerable kids and say — it doesn't matter, be yourself. She never let the cancer control her. She always kept moving forward."

Be open to the fact that you can be mentored by what you observe, take in, and assimilate. It can all be used for a greater purpose — the purpose you can envision and devise. Be open to the fact that information can come from many different directions — and as Pat King's grandfather suggested — uncover the gift in it. How often have you done that, taken a step back when someone said something thought-provoking to you, or something happened that was not what you expected? Ask yourself, what's the gift here? By allowing someone or something to offer guidance, it is always possible to learn something, but more than that, we become capable of personal expansion.

**Guidance From Within**

Ask yourself, what am I feeling? What am I thinking?

How do you feel and think about what you are doing? Tune into that and let it guide you. Does it feel good and enriching, or is it draining you? As Monica Willard of the United Religions Initiative at the United Nations states, "I do believe very, very strongly in guidance. I think we have to learn how to see those guides — those guiding lights. I just think that there is a certain level of going with the flow and following your dream that should give you enough back — that regardless of how hard you have to work, it's still worth it."

If you have a "feeling" that you should do something and the interest to pursue it, know that you are being guided to it and *just do it*. This is where your intuition, your gut, your angels — whatever you want to call it — comes in. However, that instinct will guide you to the right and perfect people, places, and things you will need to fulfill your passion. Learn to listen. Expect it to lead you where you need to go — the next step.

## A Few Questions

There is the opportunity to learn from your experiences — in other words, finding the gift of knowledge that life has taught you. Go within and ask yourself these questions:

- Who has always been there for you? Who gives you unconditional love? Who reserves judgment?
- Who are some of the people who have influenced you — a parent, grandparent, uncle, aunt, a teacher, a coach, supervisor, friend, sibling, a child? Wisdom is imparted from many different places and many different ways.
- What if you looked at everyone, every circumstance or experience in your life as your teacher — regardless of how you felt about the person or event? What could you learn?
- What do you learn every day? What experiences show up to teach you what is happening in your life and the lives of those around you? Does it move you? Does it make you think? Can you think of where you are now as sort of attending planet Earth school? Translate your everyday experiences into some of the knowledge you need to launch your dream.

We just want to say that many of the women we spoke with became role models or mentors for other people. We have learned so much from them in the development of this book. Take a moment to think about that. No relationship is linear. They are all fluid, flexible, and changeable, and you have the opportunity to learn different things at different times.

## A Good Place to Start

No matter who you are or where you live, the Internet is accessible to you. You will want to become very good friends with this avenue of information as it will give you more networking contacts than anything else. It is both ubiquitous and indispensable to you, having "offices" in almost every home in the country. The Internet can be of great assistance, allowing you to venture forth with a request — if you get no response, you've lost nothing.

Check it out for online newsletters or chat rooms for people who might be in line with your vision. You never know what will come of this, outside of useful information. You might find a support group or even a partner to share the vision with. If you have never used this online search engine, or not used it to perform specific research, go to www.google.com. Learn to use the many resources it provides to teach you how to "Google" to find everything you need.

Check out the back of this book for a great listing of all the women we interviewed and see if any are involved in an area similar to that which you wish to create, or to just look for ideas. They all provided this information for you. They are all incredible women, living their passion and walking their talk every day, all authentic spirits.

## Some Suggestions

1. Now look at your life and all those in it. Develop your own network from them. Supportive friends and family or everyday acquaintances can be a valuable resource when you are following your own vision. Many of these people will appear as you work toward developing your own passion. If you were going to start an initiative, who would you invite to your kitchen table to talk about it and help you?

2. We've stated this before, but it is so important to learn to tell people what you want to do, and why. As you focus on what you need — support, guidance, a helping hand — begin to tell people about your vision and what you are now

encountering along the way. Let them know your dream and your obstacles; you'll be pleasantly surprised how interested many are and their desire to help.

They could be the resource you need or, as more often will occur, provide you those incredible contacts that will become the resource you most need. This is a form of networking, and you should follow up on every one of these.

Many of us consider this intimidating, to reach out to those we consider strangers. But don't think of it this way. Your network should include all those you know — friends, family members, distant relatives, work associates, the acquaintances you encounter regularly on the train, at the coffee shop, your children's school, and extracurricular activities. Imagine, all those activities you are constantly playing transportation director for could now also become one of your greatest resources.

But remember, they will just as often be a contact given you from an acquaintance. When this happens, your automatic response should be "Can I use your name when I contact them?" or better yet "Could you provide an introduction?" Then follow up with this contact as soon as possible.

Then you become a friend of a friend and will not only get a response, but most likely assistance from this new source if they are in a place to provide it. If you are contacting them directly, always say up front, " My friend _____ told me I should contact you," as this will lend you credibility. Then succinctly give them your "Hollywood pitch" and let them know why you are contacting them. Never say you are hoping to "brainstorm" with them or "pick their brain." Let them know you value their time and have specific questions to ask them. This tells someone you don't plan on wasting their time and are serious about meeting them. If possible, try to meet them in person or, worst case, on the phone.

Try not to ever simply send questions through the Internet. Your contact will do so much more than give you an opportunity to ask questions; it starts a relationship with a potential source or ally. From this could come a chance to reciprocate your knowledge and experience or develop a deeper relationship, allowing you to call again down the line. This new contact will remember you more and in the future might send you other resources, or remember your vision when they encounter someone or something similar they think could assist you. Email is not a way to build a relationship.

No matter what occurs, always remember to be grateful, say thank you, of course, but later that day drop a note or an email again thanking them for their time. If you had promised to provide something or information to them, or they were to get something to you, mention it within this note.

3. Also keep a record of these new contacts, what they showed an interest in, and what was discussed. Down the road you might want to let everyone know how your project is progressing, for marketing purposes or just to stay in touch.

## A Cautionary Note

Although we don't want to contradict ourselves about talking to almost anyone, we do add a caveat about being careful who you tell your vision or your dream to early on. Look for those people you think will support you. It is important to surround yourself with others who think the way you do, who have the same desires and vision. Share with people who can share your dream. When you have a passion, honor it, go for it, and don't let anyone talk you out of it.

Sometimes you will encounter those who will try to belittle your vision or efforts, not always for spiteful reasons, but perhaps they're not living their dream. Your pursuing yours reminds them they are not doing what they love. Or maybe they are simply overprotective. Chellie Campbell recommends that you think: "Perhaps they are really angels in disguise, whose mission is to make you angry, to goad you, to create the cement that will glue you to your dream with grit, determination, and power."

Remember that a mentor, a role model, or an experience is there to teach you something. However, the message is for you. What you do with it is up to you. It is still your life, and you are the one living it. Consider what may be your unique gift, your unique contribution — no one can execute your vision the same way you can. Learn and imprint it upon your spirit.

# *Chapter Seven*
## Funding: Investment In Your Vision

*I only do what I love and I draw people to me
who do what they love — which is what I love —
and we all profit from doing what we love.*
~ Barbara Stanny

T here are as many ways to create sources of funding in the
world as there are people. Everyone has her own unique view
on how to raise the money she needs to start and maintain an
initiative. The great thing about women of vision is that they are not
only creative in what they have chosen as their path, they are creative
in the ways they produce funding for that path. But first you must
decide what it is you want and what it is worth to you. And you have
to learn to release all the "have to's" that are ringing in your head.

**What Is It Worth**

When you begin to think about it, the reality is there is no security
— other than the security you create yourself in your own mind.
Chellie Campbell points out: "...there is no insurance program that
absolutely protects you from life. There is no security; people are
always looking for security and making choices in their life to not go
for their dream, not go for their passion, in order to have this hang-on
sense of security. But security is a myth; you can lose it in an instant.
There's not a house that can't burn down, a stock that can't lose its
value, a job you can't be fired from, or your life that you can't lose
tonight. You just have to live free and be happy right now."

We admit that every vision does require *some* kind of funding. However, it is important to realize that you are only limited by your own imagination. Women have started websites, written books, given lectures, created advisory councils, worked for a company and created their vision on the side, created a company to fund their vision, or found a job that coincided with their vision and got paid. Of the women we interviewed, thirteen either started their own for-profit business, or have a business that allows them to fund their vision. Seven of them started their own nonprofit organization that now pays them a partial or full salary. One woman got her company to fund her initiative; four more are employed by a company that is the embodiment of their dream and are paid a salary; three are retired and it is that which funds their vision, while two of them are students, building their vision "on the side." You have to decide the best plan or method for you, but we would like to offer some ideas to start you thinking about how you can fund whatever initiative you might have.

## In-Kind

There are a lot of traditional ways of raising money or getting help. Kate Atwood talked to us about the new philanthropy that she envisions. In addition to actual money, she believes there needs to be a whole new shift in the *value* of volunteerism. Money is important. People will always give more from their checkbooks than time or a product or skill, but voice is important, time and service are important, and sweat equity is just as valuable. And philanthropy is evolving; it's shifting — people want to be involved — so your passion could create the opportunity for others to see their passions come to fruition.

Laura White began her operation under the auspices of another nonprofit. She has since begun her own nonprofit and set up her own board, but she still uses a lot of in-kind donations for *Wild and Water*. Pool facilities have donated pool time so that the low-income kids she works with can swim for free. She has asked other competitive swimmers her age to volunteer as teachers. She has arranged for buses from the housing communities where these kids live in order to get them to the classes. It has been a matter of coordination for her. She does do a lot of simple fund-raising activities, like selling ice cream during summer swim meets.

Laura also likes to think of herself as a Renaissance Volunteer. In addition to her own initiative, *Wild and Water,* she has coordinated efforts on a project called the *Dream Prom Project.* Her team gets people to donate money for shoes and dresses, but also in-kind donations of hair services, nail services, even a limo — so that economically deprived senior high school girls can attend their dream prom.

Heidi Kuhn, *Roots of Peace,* started out getting people to make donations in-kind. As a newsperson, she had interviewed Francis Ford Coppola when his movie *Dracula* was released. So, when she had her original reception for the landmine cause, she called him and simply *asked* him to donate several cases of wine.

Margot Swann directs a Divorce Survival School three times a year — a weekend retreat for women going through divorce. She uses women from previous retreats who volunteer their time to make the weekend as comfortable and efficient as possible — they do all the setup and clean up and cook all the meals, facilitating the ease of the experience for all involved.

Becky Douglas attracts volunteers who have to pay their own way to India and then their lodging when they get there! It's become so popular, she now has a waiting list. She even receives complaints from families when they have waited too long to apply and are put on the waiting list! How can you measure that kind of contribution?

Laura White's advice is to "Be bold!" and ask for what you want. She simply and clearly states that she's not afraid to talk to anybody about anything. When she wanted to create awards for her swimmers in *Wild and Water,* she came up with the idea to reward the best behaved swim group with a party at a Build-A-Bear Workshop — a lot of the children she works with don't have any stuffed animals. She searched online and found the CEO of the company and emailed her. Everyone in her circle of friends thought it was extremely unlikely that she would even get a response. But she did, and she got the party sponsored, and all the kids in the group got their stuffed animals. As Laura says: "You just have to ask — people are impressed by people being bold, I think. You have to let them know that what you're doing is a good cause — who you are and what you're doing. Then there shouldn't be anything to be scared of."

There are people out there with the resources and the interest in what you may want to do. And there are ways to find them. A great resource is www.Idealist.org, which is a database and website where you can find all kinds of volunteer opportunities. It also lists events such as volunteer fairs in your area, as well as educational opportunities.

## Simply Ask

That said, we know every passion needs funding. And every woman had to start somewhere. And that somewhere was with the question: Who's going to give me money? The answer comes in many ways, but it is more important what and why the question is being asked rather than how it's going to come to you. Many of the women we talked to started out by asking for help — from friends, relatives, coworkers, or even the company where they were employed.

Becky Douglas started out by inviting twenty people to her house, showing them a slide show made of the pictures she had taken in India, and asking them to sponsor one child. She was hoping that she would raise enough money for two or three children. All twenty agreed to sponsor a child. Becky thinks in today's society there is so much affluence that people are looking for meaning; because there is no meaning in affluence. We are all looking for something that makes us feel meaningful and the opportunity to give with passion.

Kate Atwood wanted to take a group of kids who had lost a parent or a sibling to the circus. At the time, her day job was in the sports industry, so she threw together a little fund-raiser at a sports bar — very informal — and her friends and the patrons raised $2,000 to get her started.

Stephanie Nelson, The Coupon Mom™, willingly admits to her frugality and created a system when she was starting out that wasn't making money per se, but she was able to *save* money in a really concrete way. She points out there are lots of ways to save money when you are starting out. She works out of her home and until six months ago used an old kitchen table as a desk. She states: "So you don't need a desk, and you don't need stationery, and you don't need a business card, and you don't need a logo. But, those are the things people go out and get first! I'm pretty successful, and I've never done any of those things. People keep asking, when are you going to have a logo done? I don't know. Is it getting in the way?" She suggests you think frugally, too. Is there a way you could spend less money? Is there a way you can use manpower? Is there a way you can use your own time? Is there a way you can get volunteers? Stephanie asks, "Is there a way you can avoid having any financial investment, because any financial investment is going to put time pressure on this..." If you are looking to save money in your endeavor, her website, www.couponmom.com, will give you lots of ideas.

## Grants

*USA Today* reviewed the book *Richistan* by Robert Frank. The article pointed out that "from 1995 to 2003, millionaires in America doubled. The new rich have a different approach to philanthropy that might in fact make big waves — instead of donating money to major charities with sizeable overhead costs, many of the new rich have devoted the second part of their careers to running their own philanthropies based on business principles — same as for-profit organizations."

If you have a vision, chances are somewhere, somebody else has a similar passion, and there have been organizations that recognize this and have funds to support it — it might be just a little bit or it might be a lot, but it is a place to start. You can search for grants at The Foundation Center, www.foundationcenter.org, and take webinars on how to apply for specific grants that you find. For example, if you live in Atlanta, www.Idealist.org will inform you each week of free educational opportunities through The Foundation Center, to support your initiative financially.

Go to your local library and work with one of the research librarians. There are directories filled with grant resources for individuals and women. You can hire a grant writer, which may be outside your budget, or you can just learn to do it yourself. As you grow, you will attract more resources to you and make your organization or passion more interesting to foundations and companies that fund the kinds of things you like to do.

Heidi Kuhn started *Roots of Peace* with a lot of sweat equity. She ran it herself for many years from her basement. She did not draw any salary at first, finding ways to cover expenses on her own. Her first grant came in for $15,000 from the *Open Society Institute* and George Soros. It was a huge breakthrough for her. Today her husband has left his six-figure job to be executive director, and they have six full-time employees in the US and three hundred employees outside of the US. Today she does draw a salary, and her organization funds her expenses.

When Andrea Shelton, *Heartbound Ministries,* started out, her first donation was $50 from her mother. She was thrilled. She acknowledges that for her vision, prison ministry, there are not a lot of corporations out there interested in that population. But a few days before Christmas 2007, she got a call. She was told that there was a man in Texas who was interested in her ministry and would like to give some money. Would she send him a copy of her budget? Andrea freely admits she does the budget herself, and it's not the prettiest budget anyone has ever seen, but she agreed to email it. Two days later she got another call and was asked for the wiring number to her bank. He was going to send her $50,000. To this day, she doesn't know the person who sent the money or how he came to know about what she was doing. But she never had to fill out a grant application or ask for the money.


## Fund Yourself

If your passion is to create an organization, think about funding it yourself. Work at another job to support it until you can support yourself, or find a job that allows you to fulfill your vision.

It took Kate Atwood three years to realize *Kate's Club,* because a shift in thinking had to take place — the idea that if something is a charity or a nonprofit, you may think that you can't have a *job* with it! She originally worked at it part-time, on the side, until she felt she could support herself through the 501(c)3. Today, she fully admits that she probably doesn't make the same amount of money as her counterparts in private industry, but she has a healthy career and would not trade what she does with any of her contemporaries.

Kathy Headlee learned just about everything she needed to know while working for another nonprofit organization. It was a wonderful way to explore and discover the business and the ways in which things were traditionally and not so traditionally done. She learned what worked, so when she started *Mothers Without Borders,* her own nonprofit, she was well grounded from the beginning. As a single mom, she needed an income, and continued to work for years at that other nonprofit job until *Mothers Without Borders* was at a point where it could pay her a salary, and then she switched over.

Serena Woolrich had a career in the federal government. For the first twenty years, she enjoyed her work and developed her initiative on the side — sometimes working thirty hours a week developing her online community. She transferred to another agency within the government for the last year and a half of her career, and *hated* it. She finally retired last year and threw herself into her work at *Allgenerations* — with her retirement funding her ability to now work full-time on her dream. She has a board of directors and is now looking into grant writing and expansion — something she just didn't have time for when she was working. In Serena's own words, "The cut and dry pattern you hear is follow your passion — well, that's all nice, but you have to pay your mortgage and do other things, too. Whatever you can do to try and retire early, do it. Then you can do something you like. Don't wake up some morning realizing that you're working just to pay your mortgage. What's the point? What a gift it is to do what you *like* every day."

For Carolyn Miller it was much the same. She recently retired after working for Bellsouth for over twenty years. She went back to do consulting work in 2007 to save extra money. She plans to use the money to fund her trip across the country, seeking out images and photographing them for her concept of *Bridges of Humanity* — and eventually produce a book. She took a year to get her finances in order so she can do what she wants.

We also urge you to consider the example set by Janine Bolon. As a biochemist, Janine chose to leave the corporate world in order to raise her children. Her family's income dropped forty-six percent, and she went from running a quarter-of-a-million-dollar laboratory, with fifteen people and twenty-six robots that ran twenty-four/seven, to caring for...one infant. After extensive research, she came up with a plan that not only could fund the family, but allow her husband to retire within fourteen years. Because they stuck to her plan, he retired in seven. She was then able to fund her initiatives. To find out more about how Janine did it, visit her website at www.smartcentsinc.com or check out her book, *Money...It's Not Just For Rich People!*

Finally, several of the women have created websites, not just for information purposes and solicitation, but actually to make money — online advertising sales and e-commerce resources help them fund their work. To see an example of this, visit Stephanie Nelson's website, www.couponmom.com. She uses sponsored ads on her site as a funding resource so that she can keep the site itself free to users.

**Sponsorship**

Sandra Clarke, founder of *No One Dies Alone*, was able to convince the hospital where she worked to develop her program and run it through their operations. They were able to do this at very low cost. Sandra had no desire to make money from this program and, thanks to the hospital, had no need to develop a foundation or nonprofit organization. Sacred Heart Medical Center in Eugene, Oregon also offers a guide and other elements of the program to hospitals around the country, again with no profit taken. This has allowed the program to spread quickly throughout the United States and now, in several other countries. This is a great example of starting your initiative within your own company, allowing you to move directly into development of the program.

Becky Douglas and Monica Willard are both funded in part by their husbands. As Becky says: "I'm lucky that he makes enough money to help support some of this. To this day he pays all my travel expenses — I've been to India twenty-three times — and granted, not everybody can do that. For me, that was just a huge benefit that someone could pay my travel expenses, but I know people have done it without that. What you do in that case, you take money out of the

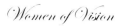

donations that come in."

For Monica, while she does receive a subsidy from the *United Religions Initiative*, she finds that her expenses exceed that stipend and admits, for the most part, "I charge it and we pay for it." Her husband travels a great deal for his work, and she uses his frequent flyer miles when she has to travel. Both women feel grateful for the encouragement and support of their husbands.

## Inheritance

What if you received an amount of money — large or small — and invested in something you dreamed of initiating? Wouldn't this be a great way to grow your vision *and* create a wonderful memorial to the person who left you the money? The summer Liz Ireland's mother died, Liz was working at a nonprofit summer theater. She was able to donate $800 to the organization in order to fund one intern's summer stipend. It was done in memory of her mother and made her feel good, and the student really appreciated it.

## The Mystical Side of Fundraising

Pat King, *Transformational Ministries,* counsels that if you have a passion around something that you *know* in the deepest fiber of your being you're supposed to do, it will draw energy. That's what the movie *The Secret* is all about; your vision, supported by your passion, will draw money and all the resources necessary to follow through on the project.

Kathy Headlee explained this concept to us in another way. She learned the nuts and bolts of fundraising from the nonprofit organization where she was employed. She knew the statistics that if you, for instance, wrote a letter and sent it out, you would probably get a one percent return, and you should budget accordingly. So she sent out the letters, she did the phone calls, and gave the speeches. Then one day something occurred to her: "I thought: Wait a minute, this isn't about me. I need to let go of that and just be intuitive about it. And it was amazing. I did that and money really started flowing in. And I know it sounds wacky — because people would say: Well, come on, how did you really do it?"

She started "manifesting" it. She always makes sure that God, angels, the forces of the Universe — whatever you want to call it — knows what she needs – and it might be $50,000 over the next few months. She still works hard; she still puts herself out there, but only sends a letter or responds to a request for a speech when she feels inspired to take that action. And she no longer worries about the money. She says: "But I realize the thing that holds me back from having more money is me. It's my willingness or ability to *believe* that money is out there waiting to come to me." But she takes no credit for where the money comes from because she doesn't do it. She just makes sure she focuses on what she needs, and trusts that it will come to her.

These examples may sound simplistic, but these women started with what they knew and what they knew they could do. The message was clear — start with where you are. Every woman treated her vision as if it were a journey rather than a destination. What they have eventually built happened over *years*, not days. However, not one person complained about this because they all felt that the path they had taken was where they found the most joy. Each person, event, or circumstance they encountered brought them further along their path, created an adventure of sorts for them, and *that* was the point. None of them believe they are done, but are looking forward to what happens next. They believe that the money isn't the be all and end all to what they want to do, but just part of the journey in getting there.

Finally, Heidi Kuhn admits to taking a major financial hit because both she and her husband work for *Roots of Peace*. They are paid salaries, but nowhere near what they have been paid in the past. He left a very lucrative position with all kinds of benefits to become executive director of their organization, and she had been a CNN reporter in Alaska. However, she says: "But how would we ever turn our back on, to me, the most important people we've met — the farmers and the fields — to see their lives improved and the gratitude in their faces — and to know that some small effort in some small way in small intentions with *great* love can produce rose petals on fields instead of mine fields."

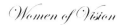

## Some Suggestions

1.  The Foundation Center is a wonderful resource with links and information about grants from virtually all the foundations in the country. They also provide educational resources for writing your grant. Visit www.foundationcenter.org. The headquarters is in New York, but there are field offices in Atlanta, Cleveland, San Francisco, and Washington, DC. There are also Cooperating Collections, which are free funding information centers in libraries, community foundations, and other nonprofit resource centers that provide a core collection of Foundation Center publications and materials. Visit www.foundationcenter.org/collections for information in your state.

2.  Another website for government funding available to you is www.usa-government-grants.org. For a minimal cost, you can have access to a wide variety of government grants, applications, and tutorials.

3.  If you're interested in learning to make money from your website, there are plenty of books and resources dedicated to this, including the bestselling *Internet Riches* by Scott Fox and *AdSense* by Joel Comm.

A cautionary note: Don't let funding, or the lack thereof, stop you in your tracks. As seventeen-year-old full-time student Laura White told us, "Well, the biggest challenge for any nonprofit, I think, is money." Yet she went on in her first eighteen months to raise $33,091.50 through a variety of fundraising sources, including grants, donations, and fund-raisers. And this does not include the in-kind donations she raised to make *Wild and Water* possible.

# Chapter Eight
## Advice: Counsel From The Sages

*We have to view success all the way. You don't reach a point of success. If you enjoy what you're doing, you are successful. If you feel like you are making a difference, if you are enjoying it, if it's exciting, you are successful from the first minute that you're doing it. Because if you think that there's some end point of success — you're never going to get to that.*
~ Stephanie Nelson

O ur interviews with these women proved they are different in so many ways, in background, education, economic status, culturally, and in how they chose their path and now follow it. What was amazing, however, was how alike they all are and, importantly, how alike their paths to success were. We noticed several themes emerging from their stories and would like to share them here.


### Aristotle Was Right...Know Thyself

Who are you? What defines you? Is it the outward things, the labels — wife, mother, account executive, vice president, CEO, teacher, butcher, baker, candlestick maker? Is that how you define your *self*? Instead of looking without, begin to look within. What feeds you? What creates your energy? What makes you feel good? Do you have what you need? Do you have what you want?

The truth is that most women don't know who they are, what that is, what they *want*, until they give themselves permission to go inside and let go of the things the outside world expects of them. Is it possible for you to take off all the costumes you wear, let go of the paradigms society expects of you as a woman, as a mother, a wife, a sister, a daughter, all of those labels? What about the expectations of others? Ask yourself: "Do I define myself based upon what my parents, siblings, teachers, coworkers, significant other, or children believe I am?"

You have the power to create yourself from a brand-new canvas. Begin your journey with yourself. Ask: "Who am I? Who am I really?" Then listen for the answer. A firm belief in your own foundation is so important because there are so many things in your life that will pull you off track.

The women we interviewed who were married and/or had children very clearly indicated that their vision belonged to them and was theirs alone. Whether or not their husbands were involved did not matter. Sometimes they caught the passion and became part of it. Regardless, for these women, their vision was theirs to begin with and remains at their core. Over and over again we got the message of the importance of doing your own thing; that whatever it is you create, start with you and what you want. Do it for the joy that it brings *you*.

Sandra Anderson, Prison Chaplain, told us: "You won't find that feeling in your life doing anything else. You just do it by faith. The older you get, the more you understand, and the more you *have* to do it." We set so many more challenges up for ourselves when we attempt to go into the outside world and start talking about peace and oneness without having that within ourselves. It just isn't possible to bypass that. It's got to be right in our own backyard first and then we start connecting the dots. As Gandhi said: "Be the change you want to see."

Monica Willard told us: "It gives me great focus. It changes my life, and as I say to people, you can't really work for peace and scream at your children. You have to be able to walk your talk." Each and every woman we spoke to does that. Each woman's vision came from a place of authenticity that was clear and lucid and second nature to her.

## What Is the Power of Your Yes

When Heidi Kuhn was asked to host the reception for those speaking on landmine issues, she didn't think; she felt, she responded, and she said YES. What is the power of your yes? What does that mean to you? When you make a commitment, how do you fulfill it? Is it obligation or joy? When you begin to find the joy of service within yourself, you have reached that point of saying yes. You do not question if you have the faith or the ability to follow it. You just respond. Your inner guidance is true and strong, and you begin to build faith around it. That is the beginning of your true path.

One of the ways you may begin to do this is by just letting go, getting your thinking out of it. At the beginning, you just have an idea of what you want to do or be, but you don't have to get caught up in the details. You don't need to think about the outcome or what form it will take.

You cannot get involved in thinking that you are powerless because you are just one person. Think about the history of the world. It could probably be written in terms of the biography of twenty or so people — women and men — Julius Caesar, Queen Elizabeth I, Joan of Arc, Abraham Lincoln, and Mahatma Ghandi. The story of the world could be told by the story of one person at a time — with a vision — who became the person for that time. None of them started out where they ended up.

Over and over we received the advice to just go ahead and start somewhere, say yes to something. If you don't know where to start — get yourself out there. Find out the needs in your own community and go and investigate. There is so much need in all kinds of different arenas. The key is to just open your eyes — something will grab you — but you've got to be looking. In addition, the first thing you enter into may or may not be for you, but it may lead to something else, or someone else who inspires, motivates, or mentors you.

## Big Packages and Small Bundles

Know that it is not necessary to have to do the "big thing." If you do small things consistently over time, it will build to great things. Just take action consistently, and keep going. Do not let the pressure of thinking you have to start big scare you out of just starting. More than anything else, that's what keeps us from starting anything. We live in a world of such extremes, and so often we come in contact with these great and grand projects or ventures, and that is where credit is given. Americans gravitate to the big, dramatic story. The truth is there are so many wonderful smaller projects that exist right now or that *you* can formulate along your way.

Kate Atwood told us: "I think we sometimes let the pressure scare us out of just starting. I think you do have to start small. I think you do have to take your big vision and bind it and level it down to a seed level. Write it down; write that down, but bring it down to a seed level. Then you'll just be empowered along the way to move forward. I do think that it is important to take the pressure off yourself. More times than not, that's what keeps us from starting anything. Through the media we're fed these huge puddles, if you will, of vision — and just like everything in life, there's different depths to it. And if you have a small puddle that's a vision, that's still as valuable as the big puddle. So don't be scared off by these big puddles."

Your vision may be big or small or even medium sized. It doesn't really matter. It may be something very small that turns out to be very big. But it doesn't have to be. It will become as big as it needs to become, so just release that pressure. Know that, accept it, and then just jump in. If you just walk across the street, you could change one person's life. As Becky Douglas explains, "It feels just as good to impact one person's life as to impact many."

## It's Just Fear

We quoted Chellie Campbell in the chapter on Fear, and it bears repeating here — she considers the downside of any risk, and if it's not death, she does it. You need to consider that kind of fearlessness about your passion. Barbara Stanny explained it to us this way: "...whenever I feel scared or terrified or anxiety or panicked, which I do a lot — I always go 'Oh goody'...because that means I'm going in the right direction. When I interviewed women for my six-figure book (*Secrets of Six-Figure Women: Surprising Strategies to Up Your Earnings and Change Your Life*), I saw that pattern. They all got to the place where they said: 'I can't do that.' And they did it anyway. They didn't even always succeed. I realized that the stretch is the pivotal point..."

We are all afraid of rejection. But this really goes back to the first question of knowing yourself. What we most worry about is disappointing those who are most significant to us, instead of being concerned that our life is significant. Oftentimes the rejection comes from those who are closest to us. Because they are concerned for our safety and security, anything out of their comfort zone will influence us. We give these people so much power. Think about keeping that power for yourself and what you want to do. We do not suggest that you never talk to people about your dream. Instead, pick people you know will be encouraging, supportive, and contributing a positive energy to what you want to do. We are so afraid of rejection. Learn to share with those people who can share your dream.

## Trust, Intuition & Vulnerability

Trust that if you are inspired to do something, then you have what it takes to do it. This is a statement of power. Know you are perfect where you are, with what you have right now. You do not need to have the platform of an Oprah Winfrey to live a life of significance, to have an impact on your world and your community. And also know that you cannot be Oprah Winfrey; she is already taken. Be you. And be the best you that you can be.

Reverend Carole O'Connell, *The Power of Choice: Ten Steps to a Joyous Life*, told us: "I know now that when there is resistance outside of me, it is mirroring resistance that I have, that I was not aware of. All those mistakes I made led me to where I am today. And the biggest gift was that I absolutely trusted that it will unfold in a right and perfect way. Trust was a big key. Trusting."

This also leads us back to the importance of our intuition. We have all heard the phrase "going with our gut," and that is well at work here. It is also going with our faith in ourselves, and our heart, and trusting that intuition that leads us on to the things that are truly important to us as the individuals we are. If a woman can reach that point within herself where she feels she has something to contribute — the way to contribute it will open to her.

Marnie Pehrson, *IdeaMarketers,* says: "I had a man comment one time that was looking at my programs: 'You have such an interesting business model. How did you come up with that?' I don't even know *what* my business model is — I just do what I feel inspired to do! A lot of times I don't have the big vision. I just do what I feel like I'm supposed to do and then I start catching the vision of it."

To a lot of people, vulnerability has a negative connotation. It smacks of weakness. Try to think of it in a different way. Instead, it is a way to open yourself up to opportunity, allowing your *self* to flow. Before it is possible to achieve anything, you must allow yourself to be vulnerable. Of course, that doesn't mean that you are not going to protect yourself against something that's not good. It means be more fluid than you are rigid.

It was this openness, this fluidity, or flexibility that has been beneficial to each of the women we talked to. It is interesting to note that no one had any huge goals carved in stone when they began. It doesn't mean that you don't create them as you go along, just that you start with where you are. It was Becky Douglas' intention at the beginning to be able to support one leper child. Now, six years later, she is very clear about eradicating leprosy by the year 2022! It was Kate Atwood's goal to take a few kids out once a month to a fun event where they could connect with others, feel better, and work through their grief. She now wants a *Kate's Club* in every community across the nation and eventually to become the voice of her generation on philanthropy!

Heidi Kuhn made a toast: "May the world go from mines to vines." At that moment, she had no idea that she would eventually have the wherewithal to clear one hundred thousand landmines in Afghanistan and put in place programs that would allow fifty thousand Afghan farmers to create vineyards rather than poppy fields. Now, she wants to put herself out of business by seeing the complete worldwide eradication of landmines!

Stephanie Nelson started with the concept of getting her circle of friends to buy groceries with coupons and donate the food to the local food pantry. Now she has four hundred and fifty thousand subscribers who use her website, and she teaches them all how to save money on their own grocery bills as well as to donate food.

None of these women started with where they are now. Instead, they went with the process, went with the journey, which brought them the resources they needed to think about those greater goals. You simply must trust that you will be empowered along the way to move forward.

## Value

It is important to recognize that each person is a valuable teacher and that it's important for us to give ourselves credence. Too many women still do not value themselves in terms of what they have to contribute to this world. They may value themselves in terms of what they do for a living, how their career has progressed, how good a housekeeper they are, or how they raise their kids. But many women do not give themselves credit for who they really are.

Beyond your passion for what you want, what are you adding to your community? We now live in a time where our community is not necessarily based on geography, but on our interests, on our passions. Ideas of community are changing so dramatically. It used to be our neighborhood. But, our communities aren't who we live next door to anymore. Our communities are those with whom we share common experiences and interests. These are the people we serve and who serve us. Jan Dahlin Geiger, *Get Your Assets in Gear!*, will never meet most of the young people she reaches through her book, but knows the impact she's having through notes and comments from them and the many people who buy it for their sons and daughters.

What skills or talents do you have that will add value to your community? How can you help? Kate Atwood said: "One of the best pieces of advice that I got was — and my vision was one of service — even if you start a for-profit company, or if you start a foundation — it's all built on your wanting to add value to your society."

## Live Now

This is it. This is all you have. There is no past. There is no future. There is only now. This is the only time in which you can make your impact. Does your time matter? Are you making it matter? What imprint are you making, and what kind of wake are you leaving for the people around you? Not yesterday, not in the future, but now, today. What does your day feel like to you? What impact does your day have on the people around you?

Over and over we heard what the Reverend Nancy Worth, Unity North Atlanta articulated: "That is one thing to share, when you have a passion, go for it, and don't let anyone talk you out of it. Go for it. What do you have to lose? All you have to lose is a life not worth living if you're not happy. You know if you're not in your bliss. I see people doing that all the time — 'Well, I have to wait until the kids graduate or I will when I retire.' And a lot of times, they retire and then can't follow their dream; they have a debilitating illness; they may even get sick and die. They don't seize the moment."

## Look for Messages

What if you took the perspective that everyone, everything had some kind of message, some kind of learning experience for you? One of the best pieces of advice we got was from Kathy Headlee, *Mothers Without Borders,* because it was simple and elegant: "Pay attention to what gets your attention." Often we get an idea from a book we read, a remark a friend makes, or something we see on television. Pay attention. If it is a message you are hearing over and over again, and each time it grabs your attention, it is a signal that your path is opening up in front of you.

Barbara Duffy's husband had a position that required them to move constantly. "It was good for me to understand that not everybody thinks the same way I do and that that's not bad. I had the opportunity to both see my way of looking at things and to open myself up to how others experience life. It was totally different for me. It was very foreign, to put it that way — it was part of our country — but it was very foreign. I think what I want to say is I lived a lot of places I would not have chosen to live. And the experience was very good for me."

Marnie Pehrson found that in her life, every time there was a major shift, it included a person who came along and gave her some information she needed, or impelled her along her path. Even when she couldn't quite formulate what it was, a person would come into her life who could help her articulate it and bring it into actuality.

Reverend Carole O'Connell was burned out as senior minister for a large church, and at that place of not knowing what to do next. She went to Florida to think things through. There was a book she wanted to read, so she stopped at a bookstore, and the woman who was running it was someone she had known previously from her work. They got to talking, and she found out that the woman was semi-retired. *Semi-retired,* thought Carole. *You can do that?* The information she received by stepping into that store altered her perspective, brought the joy back into her work, and set her on the path of what she was going to do next. This is part of the power of knowing your vision.

It is impossible to explain how we found all the women who became the basis for this book. No matter where we went, they seemed to pop up — in magazines, in conversations, through friends, while shopping — even at garage sales. We would explain what we were doing, and inevitably someone, usually someone we had not met previously, would tell us about a woman he or she knew that we just *had* to talk to.

## The Personal Challenge

That all said, know that if you choose to take the path of service, one of the pills you will have to swallow is that you are going to have to make some sacrifices. It might be financial, or social, or time-wise. If you are in a position where you have to work, then you have to find windows of time where you can work on your dream.

However, the trade-off is that if you're driven by something, you know it. It's in your gut. If you have a vision and you're hungry for it, then you will be driven. It might be hard at times, but it shouldn't be painful, and you are in control. Anything you're in control of, you should enjoy on some level.

Whatever you do, don't give up. Stephanie Nelson freely admits that if she had given up at the three-year mark, when she was sorely tempted to do so, she would never have reaped all the benefits of what became an incredible experience for her. And accept that you will make mistakes along the way; there is no way this will not happen. Consider it part of your process. But learn from them. Reverend Carole O'Connell tells us she has made a lot of mistakes over the years, but she would not go back and change even one of them. To Marnie Pehrson, it's simple: "It's very much pray for direction, get inspiration, do it."

## Some Suggestions:

1. Create what Annie Manes, *Shades of Meaning: Four Friends Facing Cancer's Challenge*, calls her "Morning Practice" — although you can do it at anytime. It includes exercise and meditation, but it could include whatever it is that you enjoy doing just for yourself. In her process, she asks herself a very direct question as part of that. "How are you?" And she waits for a response. It's not edited or premeditated; she just lets it out. And she goes with the response — which comes from a place deep within her. It is her opportunity to reaffirm her pledge to herself. What is the pledge you have made to yourself about your life?

2. Victoria Hatch, *West Wind Seminars,* suggests a three-step process for getting started. First, take time to sit and ponder the idea. Go inside and do whatever you must to receive direction in your life. For her, that's getting out in nature. Second, find mentors — people who have walked in the direction you wish to go. This will help you avoid re-inventing the wheel. Third, once you've digested the idea and you know it's something that you can commit your time and energy to, then jump in and DO IT. As Victoria said: "A friend once said to me that so many people in this world talk about other people and their stories when what we are

missing is the ability to tell our *own* stories." Have your adventures, find your passions, and then let your life be the story that you share with the world. Don't fear it — jump in and go.

3.  Become aware of your vocabulary and your self-talk. As Andrea Shelton says: "... just take the words 'I can't' out of your vocabulary. Because if I can do it, I really believe anybody can do it. And I still have to take the words 'I can't' out of my vocabulary because sometimes it just slips in."

Overall, we want to encourage you that if you have a dream, if there is something you want to initiate in your life, go for it fearlessly. If it is in you to choose to live a life of significance, the only way to do it is to move in the direction of that dream, walk it every day, talk about it with those you trust, and feel the joy that comes from being in that place of believing and creating. There is no experience like it.

## ROI: The Greatest Gift

*Where do you weigh cost vs. return on
investment in the footsteps you leave behind?*
~ Heidi Kuhn

L et's spend some time on the really fun stuff — the part that
brings joy into your life, or maybe the part that demonstrates
the joy from your life. We call this the return on your investment,
your personal ROI. This is not a financial return, but the return that
sends your spirit soaring, has you sleeping soundly at night, and
answers the question at the end of your book of days. Yes! I had a
most fabulous life.

One theme was a constant with all the interviews we conducted;
all these women had such joy in their lives. No matter what trials
they faced or daily nuisances they dealt with, they had a smile on
their face at the end of their day because of what they were creating.
Or perhaps it came from the knowledge of all the lives they were
impacting. Or, it was because they knew they could always say, "I'm
a part of the solution!" They knew they had found the key to living
their lives with purpose, on purpose.

### In Their Own Words

But don't take our word on this. We invite you to read some of
the comments from the women themselves, how they feel about what
they are doing, and how it has altered and enriched their lives.

**Heidi Kuhn, *Roots of Peace*:** "Going to sleep at night knowing that I see the footsteps, somebody that I'll never meet, perhaps never know — but that one footstep may have been saved because of the efforts and the many challenges that I faced within my day. That one footstep has been saved. And that's a legacy. That is my return. That makes it all worthwhile."

**Monica Willard,** *United Religions Initiative,* **United Nations NGO Representative**: "I know I've had the gift of being able to bring the spirit of peace more alive and very vivid to the United Nations. I meet amazing people from all over the world and it's such a joy. I cannot envision my life without it."

**Barbara Duffy, Executive Director, Fulton County Community Charities**: "Oh it has enriched me enormously. I consider myself extremely lucky to have something that makes me so full and grateful for the opportunity to be here. It is very basic, very immediate, and it has led to much satisfaction."

**Carolyn Miller, Photographer**: "The greater happiness comes from those intrinsic experiences, those things that have nothing to do with money. I have actually been touched by every one of the people that I have photographed in some way. It has forced me to look more closely at where I place my energy in the terms of my time and what value I am bringing to the world."

**Kate Atwood,** *Kate's Club*: "If I didn't have people around me, building me up by extending me to them — that's the irony here — is that by extending myself to other people, they ultimately build me up. And that's prosperity. I can't think of anything else that would fuel you in life."

**Wendy Daly, Owner, w daly salon and spa, Founder of** *Indigo Sky*: "Through all these things, it's kind of made me think about what we are doing. You've got to do something, you need to make a living, but how about make a living and really create beauty around you and in everything you do? I was very much influenced by David Wagner's book *Life as a Daymaker: How to Change the World by Simply Making Someone's Day*. His philosophy is that he is a Daymaker; it is his intention to make someone's day every day. I want our touch to be powerful and to make great days for our clients, and our company to be powerful and make greater lives for other women."

**Annie Manes, Cancer Survivor and Author:** "It was a way of feeling that we had left something tangible for people to pick up and look at. That we had made — that we turned a negative into a positive because I tried really hard to do that. I tried to find a way of turning it around so that it isn't such a negative aspect to me but that it becomes a positive one. If you read any books by people who have had cancer — they'll say it was a gift. For me, it was more than that because it was an awakening to my personal needs — as far as my body is concerned. I've learned the importance of learning to love myself."

**Reverend Nancy Worth, Senior Minister at Unity North Atlanta:** "I love the Sunday messages and working with the people in the congregation. I'm passionate about that, when I'm up in front of the crowd and sharing the message. During the week I have all the mundane details you must deal with in the running of a large church. But I love watching the life light up in someone's eyes. It's especially gratifying when someone speaks to me after a service and tells me how they had been listening and it changed their mind about their life, how appreciative they are, and they now felt that life is so much better. That's why I'm here, what I'm passionate about, and why I want to give them my best."

**Tricia Molloy, Professional Speaker, Business Consultant, and Author of *Divine Wisdom at Work:*** "I am so on purpose and I am doing something that makes a difference, for that individual, for their family, for their company, the community. It just has this tremendous ripple effect as each person recognizes their power and makes conscious choices and is aware of what their opportunities are. I feel so blessed that I can do that. To make a difference, to know that your life matters. And what I love about where I am is that I am living it, I am not only teaching it. In some cases, people are living it and inspiring others, but they are not necessarily teaching it because they are living a different role — whatever that purpose is. But for me to be able to live it and teach it and inspire it is simply divine."

**Reverend Carole O'Connell, Author, Professional Speaker & Life Coach**: "I found my passion, found my philosophy that helped me accept me the way I am, helped me to stop judging others, recognize that I am more than just my physical body. The philosophy was so transformational in my life that it changed my life forever.

The most natural thing in the world, as it was happening, I wanted to share it with others. So then the biggest change was to take that passion and make it my life work. And when I went into ministry, I didn't do it to save souls because I didn't believe souls need saving. I went into ministry because my passion was the philosophy, and I wanted to live it every day. So I would always be forced to move forward, to stretch me."

**Janine Bolon, Founder of *SmartCents, Inc.*:** "The biggest transformation has been the circle of influence created. It has dramatically increased, and I get to share in the joys. I also have a few sorrows I have to pray about and take on, but their joy far exceeds, and that is worth every sacrificed moment."

**Chellie Campbell, Founder, *Stress Reduction Workshop*:** "But also, there is something about teaching others that when they blossom they win, and every week of the eight-week program we start off with who had a win this week. When people win big in ways they never thought they would — it feels like it happened to you. I take it in as though this were my win. I love group wins. And when you help somebody else get out of losing and into winning, man, it feels good. You just so multiply your own happiness that way."

**Sandra Anderson, Doctoral Candidate and Certified Prison Chaplain:** "My passion is the prison. That's the thing that will pay me the least amount of money, but when I'm there — I'm almost their hope. You don't know what it's like after you've done twenty years of time and everybody's forgotten you. So the people that go into a prison, they are those people's family. They look to me as having not forgotten them. That's why I'm driven."

**Sandra Clarke, *No One Dies Alone:*** "One of the beauties of the program is that hospital employees and volunteers who heretofore didn't understand their connection to the patients — kitchen workers or engineers, or whatever — once they become a NODO volunteer they say, 'Gosh, now I know what we do here. I know what this is about.' The patient has the benefit of having a companion when they most need one; the nurse has the peace of mind knowing his/her patient is not going to be alone; the volunteer gets spiritual value — you could call it psychic income — from being present. Everybody wins."

**Becky Douglas, *Rising Star Outreach*:** "One day, one of the doctors we work with came to me and said: 'Becky, I want you to come down, I want you to see a patient I met this morning. I took over five hundred maggots out of this man's foot.' It was unbelievably gross. As I left that night, he (the patient) gave me the Hindu salute: 'I thank you in the name of my wife and my children and my gods. You've saved my life.' I remember when I got outside I asked that doctor if he was going to be able to save that man's foot — and he said: 'I give him a fifty-fifty chance.'

"Well, he did end up keeping his foot, and I remember that night thinking: *Dang! I love my job. I LOVE what I do!* Nothing can be more rewarding than what I do. I meet people from every level of society, and I feel like every one increases me as a person, as a human being. Before, when I was in the streets of India and saw those people, I felt powerless. It felt like it was a problem so big that there was nothing I could do, except not look. Now when I see the beggars on the street I think, *If I do my job right, hey, I'll get to you... You're going to have a better life, and you're going to feel good about yourself.*"

## The Gift That Keeps on Giving

But their gift is so much more. The gift these women also give to the world is enormous, and impacts all our lives. By our estimates, from the numbers we gathered in our interviews with just these women, the lives enriched directly number in the tens of thousands, in all fifty of the United States, in India, Afghanistan, Africa, Romania, Angola, Cambodia, Croatia, Bosnia, Iraq, and other countries. The influence on the lives further enhanced by those they touched is enormous. The positive impact on the world is immeasurable.

And this is just through the women we introduced you to here. How many others are out there we didn't interview? Because we went looking for them, we now continually hear about other women doing all kinds of things — impacting the world in many different ways. All of them have several things in common on their individual journeys: following their own passions, listening to their inner guidance, and taking inspired action to move their dream forward.

And how many more are just now finding their own voice, their vision?

When you think about it, this earth is in pretty good hands because of women of vision. But there is always room for more. We live in an ever expanding world, and the needs of that world changes and evolves just as our ideas for what we can do, be, or have change and evolve. If you have an idea, if you are pushed to expand to become a greater you, there is an obligation to step up and share that vision of yourself and what you can do for the greater expansion of our world as a positive place to live. As Andrea Shelton put it: "If we didn't have people with vision, where would we be? We wouldn't have light bulbs!"

But you rarely find women of vision in the newspaper; the daily news isn't going to highlight it. For some reason the business end of journalism doesn't believe the good stuff can attract an audience. But don't you feel better knowing they're out there, ordinary women doing incredible work, living extraordinary lives (and yes, men too, but that's another book)? Isn't it nice to stop and think, if only for a moment, that the lives these women have touched in the last few years alone outnumber all those killed in the wars you did read and hear about over those same years?

Now multiply that by all the others out there we haven't yet met. And we know they're there, many, many more of them.

How about you?

## The Personal Gift

What a joy this journey has been for us. It was our intention from the very beginning that we would become, in our own way, a small part of what each of these women was creating. And we met incredible women.

We got to work together on a creative project that has been close to our hearts, *and* we also did it with our best friend. Almost every experience that was outlined in our interviews happened to us. The synchronicity of people, places, and events was amazing to behold. From the incredible support of family and friends, the curiosity of all those new acquaintances we met along the way, and the freedom of spending eighteen months redirecting our own paths, every step of the way was fun, and we reveled in the joy of the process. What better experience is there than that?

We hope this has been helpful for you, that you have found inspiration and perhaps a little motivation to find, or expand, your personal path. Your greatest life is truly in your hands — it's been there all along. Take your first steps and remember to keep your vision ever clear in your mind; then simply follow the baby steps — no matter how small or large. They all lead in the same direction.

The joy is in the journey.

Liz and Kathleen
September 2008

We are always looking for women of vision. We'd love to hear your story. Please email us at: info@womenofvisionproject.com.

# Chapter Ten
## Meet The Women Of Vision

*And when we let our own light shine, we unconsciously give other people permission to do the same. As we are liberated from our own fear, our presence automatically liberates others.*
~*Marianne Williamson*
***A Return To Love***

We celebrate the women who participated in the development of this book through their wisdom, time, and support. Their visions continue to enrich their communities and our world every day, in many ways.

### Sandra Anderson — Doctoral Candidate and Certified Prison Chaplain

Sandra Anderson grew up in Gary, Indiana and did not have your typical childhood, although it seemed very normal to her. She was raised by two "working" alcoholics in a home where she was number seven of nine children. There was much verbal abuse in her home and not much attention to the children. Sandra began stealing at age four, taking money from her mother's purse, candy from stores, shoplifting. By the time she was eighteen years old, she was out of control and had progressed to credit card theft. She learned to target those who had lots of money and would quickly max out their cards. She would buy things that made her feel better, items for her house, clothes — she could not articulate this to anyone, but she needed nice things constantly to feel good. She earned a nursing degree, progressed through many jobs, but lost all of them due to her stealing.

It was after moving to Georgia that Sandra began getting arrested. She would go to jail and get out, go to jail again, make bond, and get out. All the while she kept stealing. She married and had three children, but continued her habit. Her kids knew she was doing this. She stole from one of their teachers, from her doctor; she had no limits. She made sure her children had everything they wanted, primarily by theft. She was a professional hustler. In 1998, she was arrested and continued to steal while on probation. Although Sandra has above average intelligence and wanted to stop stealing, she could not stop the cycle.

Then it all came crashing down. She was working for Cagle's and got caught in a sting operation. Her husband made bail, but he was tired of it. When she got home she got on her knees, and although not religious she prayed. "Lord, save me. If you're real, I'm tired of living like hell and people talking about me and knowing what they're saying is true." That same day she was arrested again on additional charges. Only this time she could not make bail. She was shackled for the first time in her life and sentenced to prison for five years, knowing she would have to serve three. No one came to her court date — no family or friends. They were all tired of it.

In the police car, in shackles, a chaplain traveled with her and asked her if she was a Christian. When she told him yes, she had gone to church and figured once a Christian, always a Christian, he told her she was a very poor witness. Sandra went silent. She didn't like the sound of that and couldn't get it out of her head. Later while in jail in Harris County, Georgia, several women began ministering to Sandra, and she began to listen and learn.

She started praying and reading the bible regularly, really understanding it for the first time. And then a purge began. She began telling the truth, telling her husband, her family, and friends what she had done to them and others. She began to feel bad about her exploits. And she began to get sick; rising daily and reading the bible, she would then be physically ill. And then she began to sleep for the first time in a long time. And also for the first time in her life, Sandra Anderson began to feel bad for the people she had harmed.

While in prison, Sandra's sister served her with papers, taking custody of her children; Sandra lost her car and her house, all her possessions, everything she had held dear. But strangely, for the first time she had peace. She began to work with the chaplains she met and corresponded with others. She attended church daily, became the chaplain's orderly, sang in the choir. Thirteen months into her incarceration, the warden and officers began to treat her differently. They actually respected her; they called her "Church Lady."

Then came a very bad day, when she was told her ten-year-old son had died. Sandra was traumatized; she knew in her heart that it would not have happened if she had been home with him. But this tragic event was a catalyst that would lead her on her current path. She still trusted in God and knew there was a plan for everything. She clung to this belief. She attended her son's funeral and gave his eulogy. It was the first time she had spoken to these people since her incarceration and change of life and heart. She spoke of God. On the way back to prison she knew, absolutely knew, that God wanted her to preach and somehow use her life and experiences to help others. She knew her latter days were going to be different, better than the former. Six months later Sandra was released.

The day Sandra left prison she told herself and God, "The only time I'm going to come back here is to minister to the people I left here." She left prison and found herself living in a trailer, all her possessions gone, one of her beloved children dead. Everything seemed dingy and dark to Sandra that day. She had her faith and knew it would be all right. Sandra had been a thief, but now, at age forty-one, she was free to pursue a new life. Sandra was given twenty-five dollars, as all are when released from Georgia prisons. She took the only money she had, went to church that day, and donated it.

She secretly hoped to be able to become a prison chaplain. Those who had ministered to her had such an impact on her life, but she knew that might be impossible given her background. She felt guided by God to return to school, graduating magna cum laude with a bachelor's degree in Biblical Studies in 2004; then received her master's of art, cum laude, in 2006, followed by a master's of divinity in 2007, magna cum laude. While in school she met yet another prison chaplain who made it possible for her to return to the prison to minister there and also introduced her to Andrea Shelton (see Andrea's profile below). After speaking at one of Andrea's

"Chaplain Luncheons," she received thirty-seven requests to minister in prisons. She became certified but, as an ex-convict, could not be hired in the prison system for ten years. So she offered her services as a volunteer.

Currently Sandra is an online instructor for the Apex School of Theology in North Carolina and a volunteer at Teen Challenge as a mentor, but spends much time volunteering as a chaplain in prison. She waits for the day she can become a prison chaplain. That job will pay her the least amount of money, but when she is ministering to those in prison, she feels she is their hope. She now supports and ministers to the women she met in prison, and many more — thieves, murderers, and others considered by most to be the lowest in society. But Sandra knows them better than that. "I went down a path of destruction, a course of destruction; I've come to understand that it led me to the ministry — that I now have the empathy most people don't have. When I was in prison I felt unloved, but God sent people, strangers, little white ladies who couldn't even cook soul food and collard greens — but they helped me, and they did it from the heart. They didn't have to do that. When I am in prison today with the prisoners, I am their family; they look to me as not having forgotten them. That is why I'm driven."

**What's next for Sandra Anderson?** Sandra is working hard to complete her doctorate now; her vision is to become a prison chaplain and facilitate incarcerated parents knowing their children. She knows better than most how parents, especially mothers, suffer with no contact from their children, and how children suffer when their parents are locked up. It doesn't change the love that exists between parent and child. Sandra knows that no matter who your parents are or what they did, God did not make a mistake making them your parents. Just knowing they love you can have a major impact on your life.

Sandra and her husband have celebrated their thirtieth wedding anniversary, and he is now a minister working on his master's degree. She has a strong, close relationship with her two remaining children, a daughter who has a counseling degree and a master's in biblical counseling, and her son, who has completed his biblical degree and is headed into the Navy.

You can reach Sandra through:
community_biblestudy@yahoo.com

## Kate Atwood — Founder, *Kate's Club*

Kate lost her mother to breast cancer after a six-year struggle with the disease. Kate was twelve. While in college her involvement with a bereavement camp in Virginia led her to discover her own healing by finding that she could bring comfort to others who had experienced the same kind of loss. She began to recognize the importance of support after such a life-changing event.

Kate began her professional career with the Chick-Fil-A Bowl, an Atlanta-based collegiate football bowl game. In 2001, she joined The GEM Group, a global sports and entertainment marketing agency. She was leading the account team for a global corporate client and its sponsorship with NASCAR, but the greater vision of a place where kids could have fun, feel safe, and learn to cope with their grief was always calling her. In her spare time she began organizing monthly outings for children who had lost a family member, events where they could have fun and share with each other.

In 2003, Kate created and established *Kate's Club*. Today Kate runs *Kate's Club* full-time. The Club's vision is to create a world where it is okay to grieve. They provide an uplifting place where children and teens gather for free social, recreational, and emotional support programs. The *Kate's Club* approach provides grieving children and their families with an environment where they can re-engage in life and turn a potentially debilitating loss into a growth opportunity.

**What's next for Kate Atwood?** Kate becomes more and more aware of the need for support for grieving children and would like to see a *Kate's Club* in every community across the country. *Kate's Club* now has a director of operations, which gives Kate more time to devote to promoting the Club. Her long-term, large vision is to be the voice of philanthropy for her generation.

You can reach Kate and *Kate's Club* through:
www.katesclub.org or info@katesclub.org
Phone: 770-618-4474

## Darlene S. Ballard — Founder, *God's Rose,* Author, Speaker, and Storyteller

Darlene launched *God's Rose*, a Christian organization, to focus on the power God has to turn a life of devastation into a life of restoration. This message of hope is delivered through Darlene's storytelling performances at prisons, churches, shelters, and other organizations.

She has also written a book of the same name, which tells about her own battles with rejection and depression, and her ultimate redemption through faith. Since 1997, over fifteen thousand copies of *God's Rose* books and audiotapes have been distributed, without profit, to prisons, community centers, shelters, and missions as well as the New York Firefighters 9-11 Disaster Relief Fund, New York Police and Fire Widows and Children's Benefit Fund, Twin Towers Fund, and The Survivor's Fund of the Community Foundation of the National Capital Region. Darlene has received thousands of letters telling her how great an impact her work has had on the lives of those who have received her book.

Darlene's book, *God's Rose*, has led to her inclusion in *Who's Who in America*, 55th Edition; *Who's Who of American Women*, 22nd Edition 2000-2001; and *The Millennium Edition of the Marquis Who's Who in the World*, 17th Edition.

**What's next For Darlene Ballard?** Darlene was employed full-time while she developed and performed *God's Rose*. She recently finished another book, entitled: *Love of a Different Kind*. She hopes to eventually move into working on her ministry full-time.

You can reach Darlene through:
www.GodsRose.org
Telephone: 334.298.5609

## Janine Bolon — Founder, *SmartCents, Inc.*

A true geek, nothing makes Janine happier than spending whole semesters describing the nature of pi, zero, and probabilities to eager young minds. Ten years ago she and her husband were both employed in corporate America, living the DINK (dual-income-no-kids) lifestyle to the fullest. A midlife pregnancy (the first of four) was the catalyst for her leaving her corporate career in biochemistry, which resulted in the family's income being cut almost in half. It was at this point that she came across some fundamental principles about money, and her vision became to design a plan for her family whereby they could accumulate wealth and financial independence.

She wanted to have enough assets so that her husband could retire from corporate life in fourteen years. It happened in seven. Since then it has become her mission to help other families collect wealth by mentoring them in the same concepts she developed for her family. She created *SmartCents, Inc.*, a company dedicated to spreading the essential principles of wealth accumulation and financial independence to all. Janine's goal is to support her clients by helping them change their views on money, learn new habits of wealth accumulation, and start walking a time-tried path to financial independence. The author of several books, including *Money...It's Not Just for Rich People!* outlining her concepts, Janine also regularly offers seminars on financial independence.

**What's next for Janine Bolon?** Janine and her family are moving to Longmont, Colorado in August, 2008 where she will be presenting her debt-free living lectures all over the state to corporations, colleges, and charter schools. She will also be working with the e-zine, *The Dollar Stretcher* (www.stretcher.com), to create a seminar series and articles for college students to learn how to pay off their debt and invest wisely to protect their future.

You can reach Janine and *SmartCents Inc.* through: www.SmartCentsInc.com or themoneymuse@gmail.com

**Chellie Campbell — Creator, *Financial Stress Reduction Workshops* and Author** (including *The Wealthy Spirit: Daily Affirmations for Financial Stress Reduction:* and *Zero to Zillionaire: 8 Foolproof Steps to Financial Peace of Mind)*

Chellie began her career as a professional actor, singer, and dancer in California. She then moved into the business world, running a small bookkeeping service, tripling its business and buying out her partners before selling the business in 1995. During the late 1980s as the recession gripped California, Chellie herself had a major financial crisis that would lead to her declaring bankruptcy and losing her home to foreclosure all in the same year. She knew it was time to regroup, and realized that she had been operating with very dysfunctional views about money. According to Chellie, this was the best thing that ever happened to her. She began to retool her thinking about personal finance, teaching herself financial principles that enabled her to pay off every debtor. She also began meeting many others in the same situation.

After counseling several acquaintances on how to put their financial lives back together and change their own views on money, one suggested her knowledge and experience could really benefit people who, through circumstances or dysfunctional practices, found themselves heavily in debt. Chellie wanted to help others, but knew it was most important to help them change their thinking and their lives, not just reduce their debt. A lifelong path of spiritual education partnered with her business and financial knowledge, personal experience, and performing history ultimately coalesced into her developing her own brand of coaching workshops to help others reclaim their lives.

Today Chellie supports others with her own knowledge and experience, utilizing humor and a touch of whimsy through her many speaking and radio engagements, *Financial Stress Reduction Workshops,* and her books.

**What's next for Chellie Campbell?** In 2008, Chellie launched another vision to expand her ability to reach and support others nationwide gripped by the stress and anxiety of growing debt. She began educating and coaching her first group of new program

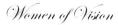

trainers to take the workshops out into several states, and plans on holding several such programs annually.

You can reach Chellie and obtain information about her *Financial Stress Reduction Workshops* through:
www.chellie.com or Chellie@chellie.com

## Sandra Clarke — Founder, *No One Dies Alone*

On a rainy night in 1986 at Sacred Heart Medical Center in Eugene, Oregon, Sandra Clarke met a man whose name she can no longer remember — a man she'll never forget. He was the first patient on her initial rounds that night, frail and old and near death, with "do not resuscitate" instructions on his chart. He asked, "Will you stay with me?" to which Sandra had to reply she would have to finish her rounds first, but would return when she could. That time arrived an hour and a half later, after completing normal tasks for other patients. When she returned, the man had died. Sandra felt awful. She knew he was going to die, and with a DNR she could not have stopped that, but he had died all alone.

For years afterward, Sandra would talk about her idea, for a program to provide all dying patients with a personal contact at the end, to friends, other nurses, and hospital administrators — all to no avail. There seemed no easy way to coordinate the program. Then came the Internet. In the year 2000, Sandra once again found herself discussing the idea with a colleague; a nearby pastoral care director overheard her and asked her to submit a proposal, which he then took to the corporate office. Sandra brought together the hospital PR director, risk management, head of volunteers, and other disciplines in the hospital to discuss all the obstacles, confidentiality concerns, and other implementation issues. *No One Dies Alone* was then launched in November 2001 with minimum expense.

*No One Dies Alone* is a volunteer program at Sacred Heart that provides the reassuring presence of a volunteer companion to dying patients who would otherwise be alone. Being present at the end of someone's life, volunteers are there to make sure patients are warm or cool, the covers are right, they're not agitated, and the room is a comforting place. With the support of the nursing staff, these companions are able to help provide patients with that most valuable of human gifts: a dignified death. For the first three and one-half years, Sandra Clarke ran the program herself to find the kinks and look for areas of improvement. Today there are six to eight phone coordinators, each working a few days weekly. The program is manned by hospital staff and hospital volunteers. Most of the patients are in the critical care or oncology units, and may include the homeless, patients whose loved ones are not in Eugene, and what Sandra calls the "elder orphans," a person who has outlived their family and friends. The benefit to dying patients is immense, but no less is that for the volunteers who feel they are making a difference in someone's life and learning valuable end of life care.

*No One Dies Alone* has its own web page on the Sacred Heart/PeaceHealth intranet where employees and hospital volunteers can sign up. Other hospitals interested in duplicating the program are provided a comprehensive guide, written by Sandra, as well as other materials to help them launch. To date, over nine hundred have been distributed around the country.

**What's next for Sandra Clarke?** Sandra hopes to soon be able to track the requests for the NODA manual to find where the program has actually launched around the country. She also sees it growing into nursing homes and hospices. Churches have voiced interest in starting their own programs; phone trees are suited to congregations, and they could support their congregants who are alone. Sandra has a strong belief in human rights, particularly when a person is most vulnerable. Her hope is in time, it may be true that *No One Dies Alone.*

You can request more information and reach Sandra through:
www.peacehealth.org/Oregon/NoOneDiesAlone.htm or
sclarke@peacehealth.org

## Wendy Daly — Owner, w daly salon spas and founder, *Indigo Sky* and *Outside In*

Originally from Hammond, Louisiana, Wendy survived an abusive childhood that forced her to leave home at fifteen. But Wendy had a passion within, coupled with a strong faith in a higher power that she knew could be counted upon to guide her where she needed to go. With the support of an aunt, Wendy completed her GED, then put herself through cosmetology school. She eventually settled in Peachtree City, Georgia with her family: a husband and three daughters.

In 2003, she opened the first of two w daly salon spas, launching her dream of providing a place where women would be nurtured and pampered. In her own words she wanted to "provide women a soft place to land in their hectic lives." Divine guidance stepped in again with the opportunity to join a church trip to Nicaragua, a trip that launched Wendy on yet another venture, one that would ultimately enable her to reach out and support women and girls, providing them some support and needed direction in their lives. After that fateful trip, Wendy began traveling to Nicaragua to share her hair styling skills as a means for women to better support themselves, their families, and villages. From this was launched her foundation, *Indigo Sky*.

Today, *Indigo Sky* supports these women from the villages of Nicaragua, sponsoring them in cosmetology school and also bringing Wendy and her salon professionals to Central America to teach their craft. In 2007, Wendy expanded *Indigo Sky* to include her local community as well, reaching out to middle school girls through a new program, *Outside In*. Wendy and other stylists provide these young girls with the best in personal care and instruction, as well as the valuable experience and wisdom of women through mentoring, all designed to build their self-esteem and confidence before entering adolescence and high school.

Wendy brought her dreams to life through her talented children, the incredible care given her salon guests, and the opportunities for girls and women everywhere to live their greatest life. Wendy and her company, w daly salon spa, are living up to their vision, providing the care, wisdom, and support for women everywhere to

**What's next for Wendy Daly?** Wendy and her staff continue to travel to and support women in Nicaragua, providing schooling, personal training, and the tools necessary to their trade. Back at home, Wendy is building *Outside In* through expanded programs and reach. In addition to the personal care and attention with her staff, they are adding fashion stylists and nutrition and etiquette classes for these girls who are found through school counselors. Each young girl is provided support through personal meetings and classes six to seven times a year. The program is also expanding in Atlanta, currently supporting young girls in two counties.

You can reach Wendy and learn more about her foundation through:
www.wdaly.com

## Becky Douglas — President, *Rising Star Outreach*

Becky is motivated by the belief that every person deserves opportunity and a life of dignity. A stay-at-home mother of nine children, her eldest daughter, Amber, was diagnosed with bipolar disorder when she was seventeen. After eight years of struggling, Amber took her own life while at college in February, 2000, devastating her family. While going through Amber's things, Becky learned that her daughter had been sending part of the money she and her husband had been providing her for college expenses to an orphanage in India. Even though Becky was surprised, it was very much in character for Amber. Since she suffered so much herself, she always seemed to have a tender spot for others who were suffering as well.

As a tribute to their daughter, concerned friends were asked to send donations to this orphanage in lieu of flowers for her funeral. So much money was sent in that the orphanage asked Becky to join their board of directors. Becky decided to travel to India to learn about the orphanage. When she got there, she was pleased to learn that the children in the orphanage were well-cared for. However, it was on the streets, going from her hotel to the orphanage and back again each day, that Becky saw suffering that changed her life forever. The leprosy-afflicted beggars on the street seemed to swarm the car at every stoplight. Their suffering was so severe, it seemed almost palpable. Becky could hardly bring herself to even look at them, their suffering was so intense.

When she returned from India, she had trouble sleeping. The images of the leprosy-affected beggars were on her mind all night. She finally decided that she could either live with insomnia forever, or she could do something about the problem that was haunting her. She gathered three friends around her kitchen table, and together they started *Rising Star Outreach*, a small charity dedicated to serving the leprosy-affected in Southern India.

In 2003, *Rising Star Outreach* was fortunate to partner with one of India's well-known social activists, Padma Venkataraman. The daughter of former India president R. Venkataraman, Padma has long been a leading figure in the national fight against leprosy and its resulting stigma. Padma was working with a micro-lending program in several colonies already, but had recently run out of money. She contacted Becky, and the two joined forces.

RSO's mission is to help the leprosy colonies of India become thriving, self-sufficient communities. This is accomplished through three major initiatives: to provide leprosy patients with their own small businesses using micro-financing; educate the colony children in a safe, healthy environment; and address the unique health challenges of the colonies with mobile medical units.

To date *Rising Star Outreach* is active in forty-five colonies. It encompasses an extensive volunteer program, a school where lower and upper caste children now learn together, and homes for orphaned children. They have been invited to come and open their program throughout India, to include the micro-lending program, various businesses in the colonies, and mobile medical clinics.

**What's next for Becky Douglas**? Students for Self-sustainable Schools, a group of six students partnered with *Rising Star Outreach*, competed in the annual Marriott School of Business Social Venture Contest with their business plan aimed at making RSO's boarding school self-sustainable within five years. They were selected as the winner of the Audience Choice contest and the overall winner as determined by the judges. The prize money will be used for implementing the program. In keeping with RSO's mission, this plan includes the construction of a traditional hotel, which will generate future streams of income from guests' room and board.

You can reach Becky and *Rising Star Outreach* through:
Amelia Humphrey, Office Manager:
ahumphrey@risingstaroutreach.org or www.risingstaroutreach.org

## Barbara Duffy, Executive Director — North Fulton Community Charities

Barbara was a corporate wife and moved with her husband to support his career eleven times in sixteen years. Finally, she and her husband decided to put down more permanent roots and raise their family of five children. Her husband shifted careers, and Barbara continued the volunteer work she had always done in whatever place they landed. She always felt it was extremely important to contribute to the community as well as to have something that belonged solely to her. She was president of the PTA and eventually ran for the local school board, becoming president and contributing her expertise at a time when severe budget cuts had to be made, and many schools were closed. Barbara served on the school board for eight years.

Her volunteer work included an organization called The Clothes Closet where she eventually served on the board of directors. Later it became necessary for her to be employed and contribute to her family's income. Luckily, her timing coincided with the expansion of The Clothes Closet into North Fulton Community Charities and the need for a director to organize and guide it. Barbara was the natural choice, and she was able to step into that position. Her passion for her work expanded into a paid position where she still works today.

North Fulton Community Charities' mission is to prevent homelessness in North Fulton County, part of metro Atlanta, by supporting families in their homes during short-term emergencies. By pooling the resources of local religious, business, and civic groups and individuals, NFCC assists families with rent, utilities, transportation, food, clothing, medicine, and other basic needs. NFCC also coordinates special assistance to families during the holidays and matches volunteers with projects.

**What's next for Barbara Duffy?** Barbara continues to work and serve her community as director at NFCC. She gives speeches and interviews on behalf of the organization and has inspired many with her dedication, including Stephanie Nelson (see below).

You can reach Barbara Duffy and the North Fulton Community Charities through: www.nfcchelp.org
Telephone: 770-640-0399

## Jan Dahlin Geiger — Certified Financial Planner, Speaker, and Author (*Get Your Assets in Gear!*)

In January of 1986, shortly after her second son was born, Jan Dahlin Geiger decided to make a major change in her life. A vice president for Citicorp in corporate banking at the time, she wanted to stop traveling and be home more often for her children. After deciding to make a change of career to do so, she began listening to self-improvement tapes, starting with those by Brian Tracy. That was when her vision began to form. Brian suggested listing goals for all aspects of your life, including "service and giving" goals. Jan gave herself an F in that category and decided then and there to find a way to do better and make it consistent by integrating it into her life's work. Jan opened herself up to service and began to connect with others. Through Margot Swann's *Visions Anew*, she lent her expertise to women going through the divorce process. Through Andrea Shelton's *Heartbound Ministries*, she taught prisoners in the Georgia penitentiary system new financial skills.

A chance conversation with a friend about young people and finance set her on her path to launch seminars educating young people in their twenties and thirties about managing money. Jan learned valuable lessons as a child from her mother that would later lead to her becoming quite wealthy. The three lessons she learned at a young age she knew most kids never learn at all. She wanted to

111

find ways to teach this to young people early in their work lives. Jan's classes revolve around these three simple guidelines: 1) remain debt free, 2) pay yourself the first ten percent of whatever you earn, 3) learn to invest wisely. Today Jan holds seminars and classes named after and based upon her book, *Get Your Assets in Gear!* to reach even greater numbers of this target audience.

Although Jan has no need to work, she does so because she loves it, and it allows her to give to causes close to her heart. She continues to speak to larger and larger groups, charging very little and donating that money to charity. Her book is now used by many people, young and not so young, and purchased as gifts by many more for graduating students.

**What's next for Jan Dahlin Geiger?** Jan has a long-range vision to get in front of millions of people and sell millions of books for the explicit purpose of empowering larger numbers of people about their money. She plans on bringing them a message of hope through humor as she teaches people how to change their relationship with money and view their money as a tool to design the life they were really meant to have. And that means television. Frequently in the media, Jan has been quoted in a number of publications, including *Wall Street Journal, Reader's Digest, Money Magazine, USA Today, SmartMoney Magazine,* and many others. She has also appeared on a number of radio and TV shows. At present, she is the financial expert for Wedding Television Network's *Love and Money,* broadcast on Comcast Cable. She plans to do more television to reach the widest possible audience with her message, her humor, and her wisdom.

You can reach Jan through:
www.getyourassetsingear.com

## G. Victoria Hatch — Director, *West Wind Seminars*

Victoria Hatch is a social entrepreneur. Born of the Ojibwe Tribe, she was raised in rural Northern Minnesota in two worlds, both the Indian and the white world. Almost six years ago, Victoria had an inspiration about building a bridge between those two worlds while alone in the mountains of Idaho. It was here that her vision was seeded, to educate herself about her heritage, the Indian culture, and combine this with a love for helping others find their worth, no matter what their circumstances. Being of two worlds would allow her to be a bridge of understanding between both, educating others and supporting Indian youth trying to find their own way. Ultimately, from this *West Wind Seminars* was created.

*West Wind Seminars* is devoted to restoring what has been lost in American Indian culture, empowering those of Indian descent to live up to their full potential, and bringing about a healing among the people, individually and as a whole. Victoria is an international speaker on topics such as indigenous/holistic education, vision, historical cycles, and healing.

**What's next for Victoria Hatch?** Victoria is working toward another conference for Native youth in Utah and hopes to make this an annual regional event to include youth all over the western region. She also plans on expanding to assist other urban areas, as well as counsel individual tribes, supporting them in developing similar conferences for their youth. Her vision is to use her experience to consult with other tribes and assist them with the complicated steps of encouraging healing within their communities.

You can reach Victoria and *West Wind Seminars* through:
www.westwindseminars.org

## Kathy Headlee, Founder — *Mothers Without Borders*

Kathy Headlee was taught by her parents to be aware of what was going on in the world and to be engaged in community service. Her family's conversations always included what was happening to other people in the world, how others lived. It was a family trait she incorporated into her own children's upbringing. She provided them with opportunities to reach outside themselves and develop an understanding of how other people lived, through community service. This focus brought her an awareness of a growing crisis for orphaned children in Romania in. In 1991, she began organizing trips for volunteers who wanted to get involved. It was during her work in the orphanages of Romania that Kathy was confronted with the devastating results of children raised without nurturing, without encouragement from caring adults, without hope. She communicated the needs of these children to others and found men and women around the world responded by offering their time, talents, and resources to alleviate the suffering of these often forgotten children. *Mothers Without Borders* was created, officially becoming a 501(c)3 in 2000, and currently working within the African nations.

More than thirty-six million children under the age of fifteen are orphaned today in Sub-Saharan Africa, and it is feared that over eighty million more are orphaned in Asia and India. Kathy realized early on that it is not feasible to institutionalize all these children. "We need to strengthen the communities so that these children can be raised in an environment where they are cared for and nurtured and have an opportunity to be educated." Early on, Kathy recognized an intriguing irony, there was an exploding segment of the world's population becoming orphans — children raised without adult care, supervision, or guidance. But there was equally an exploding population in developed countries having huge amounts of discretionary income, time, talent, and resources. Her goal was to create a bridge that would bring these two groups together, find ways to transfer these resources into those places where they need that support, then turn those communities loose to solve their own problems.

The official purpose of *Mothers Without Borders* is to "address the needs of orphaned and abandoned children in a holistic manner." The focus is on three areas: strengthen the communities and families who are actually willing to keep these orphans; empower the women in these communities through training and micro-lending, allowing them to become agents of social change; and nurture and protect the children. They support efforts to provide safe shelter, food, clean water, education, and access to caring adults. *Mothers Without Borders* wants to assure that each child has someone who cares about them and can teach them of their value.

**What's next for Kathy Headlee?** Kathy has a vision for a

project in development right now in Zambia. They are building a large training center to include a school and healing center, a vocational training center and medical clinic, as well as a women's support center. Her vision is to use this as a model to allow people from all over Zambia to come for weeks and use whatever facilities and resources they need, then send them back to their communities. Her dream is to see it replicated elsewhere through *Mothers Without Borders* or other organizations.

You can reach Kathy through: www.motherswithoutborders.org

## Pat King, Founder — *Transformational Ministries*

When Pat was three years old, her mother left her in the care of her grandparents. Her grandfather had studied Eastern religions, had been through two world wars, served in China, and was looking to find some peace. For him, the spiritual life was very important, and it wasn't about religion — it was about expanding an individual's spiritual life. Pat stuck like glue to him, and they had a wonderful relationship where she was guided, protected, and loved. She was also exposed to Eastern thought at an early age.

Years after the death of her grandfather, while cleaning out her garage, she rediscovered one of his Religious Science textbooks and began to think about her own path. She found a Religious Science church and began to take classes, eventually attending ministerial school and becoming ordained.

When her marriage ended in 1990, she left California and moved to North Carolina to co-create the first Religious Science church there, *The Center for Creative Self-Discovery.* After eight very successful years she moved to Florida and became the spiritual director of a mind-body fitness organization. In 2002, she created her own nonprofit called *Transformational Ministries* to expand the personal vision of her ministry, which is to "Spread Truth Around the World Through Love and Greater Awareness."

**What's next for Pat King?** Pat is a passionate and dynamic teacher, speaker, and spiritual intuitive who is willing to go wherever her "inner guidance" takes her in order to be the instrument of God's love and compassion. Today, she is a much sought after speaker at women's retreats and conferences around the country.

You can reach Pat King at:
1205 Pacific Hwy # 804 / San Diego, CA 92101
Phone: 619-358-9011

## Heidi Kuhn, Founder — *Roots of Peace*

When Heidi's husband was transferred from California to Alaska, they had three children, the oldest of which was five. As if that weren't enough of a change, she was shortly thereafter diagnosed with cervical cancer. It was around the Fourth of July when she had to return to California to have her medical procedures performed, and she wondered if she would even see another Fourth. Her fervent prayer was: "Dear God, grant me the gift of life that I may do something special with it." By the next Fourth she was much healthier and working for KJUD/ABC and had arranged an uplink to *Good Morning America* in New York to celebrate the place in our country where the dawn's first light hits on the Fourth — Alaska. Shortly after that she became a CNN reporter in Juneau, Alaska and was reporting on site when the Exxon Valdez ran aground in Prince William Sound, launching her into the national spotlight.

Heidi's husband subsequently took another job in California with a startup company called Adobe Systems. Once back in California, this cervical cancer survivor happily gave birth to her fourth child. While staying at home with her children, the next pivotal point in her life arrived. In 1997, she was asked to host a reception at her home for a group that planned on speaking on the landmine issue that Princess Diana had publicized. They were doing a nine-city tour culminating in the Commonwealth Club in San Francisco, and ended up being there three weeks after Princess Diana died. Heidi readily agreed to host the reception.

Heidi made a simple toast that night: "May the world go from mines to vines." That was the beginning of the development of her passion. It led her to create *Roots of Peace,* which she operated out of the basement of her home for the first five years. Her husband eventually joined her, and together they run the organization out of the US headquarters in San Francisco.

In 2007, *Roots of Peace* celebrated its tenth anniversary working to unearth dangerous landmines in war-torn countries and empower the local communities scarred by these inhumane weapons. Currently, they work to build sustainable crops on land once too dangerous to traverse in Angola, Cambodia, Croatia, Bosnia, Iraq, Afghanistan, and the Kyrgyz Republic, transforming the scars of conflict into the roots of peace.

**What's next for Heidi Kuhn?** Continually on the move, *Roots of Peace* was invited to the annual Squisito! event hosted at San Patrignano, Italy, on May 30 through June 2, 2008. Over 50,000 European guests attended to savor a "taste of peace" from countries such as Myanmar, Peru, Thailand, and Afghanistan — all through the efforts of NGO (non-governmental organization) organizations seeking to establish successful public/private partnerships to replace "seeds of terror" with "seeds of hope."

You can reach Heidi Kuhn and *Roots of Peace* through:
www.RootsofPeace.org
Roots of Peace, US Headquarters / 1299 Fourth St., Ste. 200 / San Rafael, CA 94901
Phone: 415.455.8008

**Annie Manes — Co-Author,** *Shades of Meaning: Four Friends Facing Cancer's Challenge*

Annie's dream has always been to lead a happy life. As simplistic as that may sound, it is not always easy to live that conscious decision. Her first challenge occurred when she was in her early twenties and accompanied her husband and young son in their car as they drove over a frozen lake in Minnesota to meet with friends and watch some sport fishing. The ice beneath their car cracked, sending them all into the deep, freezing water of the lake. Annie was the only survivor.

From that tragedy in her life, she was thrown into running the suburban weekly newspaper her husband had started in order to keep it going before she could sell it. A blessing in disguise, the paper provided a coping mechanism for her, requiring a great portion of her attention and causing her to focus on something besides her grief. Eventually she did sell the newspaper and ended up meeting her second husband, to whom she has been married for forty-five years.

At the age of fifty-four, she was diagnosed with stage four breast cancer, and numerous nodes were involved. It was around Thanksgiving, and she vividly remembers wondering, so much like Heidi Kuhn, if she would see another Thanksgiving. She made a conscious decision to enjoy the time she had left. So she began to take classes and do things that would take her out of the chain of feeling so different because of the cancer diagnosis. It was at one of those classes that she met a woman who suggested she join a support group at the local hospital.

Joining the support group ended up being one of the most important things she did in her life. She learned so much — not just from the woman who conducted this group, but also from the other people with cancer in the group. There was so much wisdom imparted every week that she got the idea of putting some of that wisdom on film. A video was produced of the group that was shown at various doctors' conferences.

Eventually, Annie left the group and began to think about writing a book, the intended purpose of which was to help others by what she and the group had experienced. She had met incredible women in the support group, many of whom were younger than she and who were lost to the disease, but she had written down many of the thoughts and comments that came out of the group. She asked three other members in the group to join her in writing *Shades of Meaning: Four Friends Facing Cancer's Challenge.* It was meant to be a sign of appreciation to the oncologists, nurses, and technicians who helped them through their cancer experience. It was made available to doctors' offices, libraries, and local bookstores and was a therapeutic experience for her as well as a supportive guide for many women.

**What's next for Annie Manes?** Now retired, her cancer in remission, Annie spends her time with her husband splitting the year between homes in California and Minnesota.

## Laina Maxwell, Founder — *The Center for Awareness*

The death of Laina's mother was a catalytic event in her life as it is for many of us. She had had a strained relationship with her mother and found herself feeling depressed, scared, empty, sad, and lonely. She was glad her mother had finally died, and then she felt guilty for feeling relieved.

Her life began to change when a friend suggested she attend a week-long seminar, which catapulted her into a five-year pursuit of knowledge and personal transformation. She began to read and still does, now counting her research into the hundreds of books and participation in numerous group discussions. She began to realize that she was born with a passion to teach and an understanding that as you gain awareness of the workings of your mind, it is possible to heal childhood wounds, stop the daily drama, embrace the lessons of the past, step into the present, and welcome the amazing being that will emerge.

Now trained as CTI Life Coach and Avatar Master, she has assisted clients in achieving their personal transformation by guiding them toward a level of awareness and understanding of how their mind works. She also provides them the tools with which to create the life they desire. She developed the *Power of Awareness* workshop out of her personal coaching business. Through this course she teaches how beliefs show up in fear, anger, depression, and low self-esteem. She then assists participants in gaining an awareness of how these beliefs limit their ability to create the life they desire. From this place of clarity they reclaim their power to become the creator of their life.

**What's next for Laina Maxwell?** Laina's workshops are filling up, and she is involved in more and more public speaking engagements. She is currently writing a book, *The Power of Awareness,* and developing a one-day course for children in middle school.

119

You can reach Laina Maxwell through:
www.thepowerofawareness.com

### Carolyn Miller — Photographer, *Photographic Sojourns*

Carolyn's love of photography has taken her all over the world, including South America, Canada, France, Italy, Spain, Portugal, England, Switzerland, Hong Kong, Singapore, Bangkok, Malaysia, Hawaii, the Caribbean islands, and several of the US national parks. She loves to share her work to reflect the beauty and goodness in this world, the sojourn of opening to the beauty in all elements of life.

Since retiring from her job at Bellsouth, she has been devoting much of her time to her photography. In 2006, she had her first exhibit at the Rialto Theatre in Atlanta, *Bridges of Humanity*. This was a first step to a larger work and book she is planning that demonstrates how we are all connected. "When people find a way to make a difference, they move the world into a place of higher awareness one step at a time, by touching one person at a time. In that process they are creating bridges, connecting their own path to the path that others they affect will one day walk." Her work from many formats can be found online at
www.photographicsojourns.com.

**What's next for Carolyn Miller?** Carolyn is collaborating with Nafisa Valita Sheriff on a photographic display similar to her first exhibit, *Bridges*. This exhibition will center on a group of "unsung heroes" representing the African American story. Their vision is that these day-to-day stories will raise awareness of the positive modeling currently occurring within the African American culture. The exhibit is planned for late 2009.

You can see Carolyn's work, keep up with her exhibits, and reach her through:
www.photographicsojourns.com

**Tricia Molloy — Professional Speaker, Business Consultant, and Author** (*Divine Wisdom at Work: 10 Universal Principles for Enlightened Entrepreneurs*)

Tricia started her own public relations firm, *Molloy Communications*, in 1988 to support the success of other passionate entrepreneurs. Known as "The Queen of Serene," Tricia's wise, peaceful presence and commonsense advice are welcome in today's challenging, complex business environment.

Having always utilized principles such as kindness, compassion, and integrity in her own work, she became conscious of the need to communicate the importance of these principles in the working world at large. She began to develop a system, to speak on the topic, and eventually wrote her first book.

Today, Tricia offers workshops, retreat programs, tele-seminars, and coaching, inspiring businesspeople to achieve their goals and meet the challenges and opportunities at work using these principles. She currently works with organizations such as Home Depot and the Atlanta Convention and Visitors Bureau. She has been featured in newspapers and magazines and on radio, podcasts, and television. Her most popular program, *CRAVE Your Goals!*™, presents a powerful, practical five-step system for attracting what you desire and deserve.

As she encourages others to find their life purpose and make it their life's work, Tricia is fulfilling hers, which she has articulated as: *Through support and by example, I inspire others to follow their dreams and live joyfully on purpose.*

**What's next for Tricia Molloy?** Her second book, *Take Your Higher Self to Work: 7 Best Practices for Success*, will come out in early 2009. Through her new division, *Working with Wisdom for Life!* she offers a free workshop each quarter to nonprofits that teach life management skills to the community.

You can reach Tricia Molloy and *Working with Wisdom* through: www.divinewisdomatwork.com

## Stephanie Nelson — Founder, The Coupon Mom™

In 1995, Stephanie Nelson left a career in the world of corporate sales and marketing to become a stay-at-home for her sons. Early on she figured that if she was going to keep that job, she would have to learn to be as cost conscious and budget oriented as any corporate mogul. She put a system in place to slash her grocery bills.

As part of a food drive at her church, she thought it would be a fun idea to see how many coupons she could use to buy food and donate it. She ended up purchasing sixty dollars worth of food for fifteen dollars. In October of 2000, she visited the local food pantry and discovered that the pantry shelves were empty, but the waiting room was full. To help fill their shelves, she began teaching a few friends how to buy food with coupons for that charity, which led to the launch of her own program *Cut Out Hunger.* Today, thousands of shoppers are "cutting out hunger" across the country. They donate tons of food to feed the hungry in their communities, while saving money on their own groceries as well.

By 2004, Stephanie had become known as The Coupon Mom™ and has taught television viewers and readers how to save in many areas, including travel, clothing, restaurants, groceries, gifts, theme parks, gardening, and entertainment. She has appeared frequently on national and local television and radio, teaching savings tips, including the *Today Show, CBS Early Show, CNN,* and several segments on *Good Morning America.* She writes a monthly column for *ABCNews.com.* She is the author of the book *Greatest Secrets of the Coupon Mom,* published in October 2005. Over five hundred thousand members use her free grocery deals website www.couponmom.com each month.

In 2004, the Coca-Cola Company honored the *Cut Out Hunger* program by selecting Stephanie to be a torch runner in their Athens 2004 Olympic Torch Relay. Coca-Cola selected participants for their "ability to inspire others and make a positive difference in people's lives."

**What's next for Stephanie Nelson?** Conscious of the ever escalating food prices, Stephanie is beginning to partner with major newspapers in large markets to provide free resources for people to save money on their groceries and to feed the hungry. She is writing free e-books for them, such as: *Cut Your Grocery Bill in Half with the LA Times and the Coupon Mom,* which will be printed and distributed in grocery stores in those markets.

You can contact Stephanie Nelson through:
www.couponmom.com and www.CutOutHunger.org

**Reverend Carole O'Connell — Co-founder, *Center for Creative Living*; Speaker, Life Coach, and Author** (*The Power of Choice — 10 Steps to a Joyous Life, Seven Secrets to Abundant Living,* and *The Adventures of CJ and Angel: The Scary Helicopter Ride*)

The Reverend Carole O'Connell did not have a purpose or a mission in life during her twenties and thirties, outside of her children. Admittedly she was "lost in the weeds" and unhappy. Not a religious woman, Carole nevertheless realized she was divinely inspired to pick up and move with her children from New Jersey to Florida, beginning a quest for a new chapter that would ultimately change her life, as well as many others.

Coming from a nursing background, Carole knew she wanted to be involved in healing and was also being introduced to new thought philosophy, for which she became a passionate student. This would lead Carole into unknown territory as she began a five-year quest to study and learn and develop her new role in spiritual work. During that time she took courses and seminars, studied books, and worked with other spiritual leaders. A chance opportunity to speak at a Sunday service would lead Carole into her new life. She became a Unity minister in Florida, ultimately spending over twenty-five years in ministerial work, building what would become the largest Unity church in Georgia. Additionally, in 1988, Carole co-founded the Center for Creative Living with the purpose of facilitating personal and spiritual awareness.

In 2005, Carole retired from the ministry to discover her next path along her journey, working with people individually while developing ways to reach greater numbers. Drawing on her more than twenty-five years of experience as one of the most successful

Unity ministers in the country, she teaches the universal principles of creative living. She accomplished both through a thriving life coaching practice and through her books for adults and children. Reverend Carole O'Connell is an exciting motivator of people. With humor and charm, she inspires her audience to expand their thinking, to feel more deeply, and to look at life from a higher point of view.

**What's next for Reverend Carole O'Connell?** Carole continues to work with her coaching clients and has new books in the works. She is much in demand for speaking engagements. Her first spiritual cruise to Alaska, developed with the Reverend Kathianne Lewis, took place late summer of 2008. She also plans on spending much quality time with her husband and grandchildren, including grandson CJ, on whom her children's book adventures are based.

You can reach Carole and learn more about her services and books through:
www.caroleoconnell.com

**Marnie Pehrson, Writer & Internet Entrepreneur**

Mother of six, creator of nineteen websites, Marnie Pehrson started her home business back in 1990 as a computer trainer and consultant. She wanted to be able to help support her family, and felt a strong need to also be a stay-at-home mom for her kids. Marnie loves to help people learn about and use the Internet and has a knack for explaining complicated ideas. Like the old man in Will Allen Dromgoole's poem, "The Bridge Builder" (listed in the back of this book), Marnie loves to use her talent to support other's needs. In 1994, she wrote *How to Run a Computer Training Business* and began marketing it on AOL and Compuserve. By 1996, she and a friend, Alanna Webb, opened the first online mall.

In 1998, Marnie combined her love for writing with her knack for marketing to create *IdeaMarketers.com,* which has become the longest running article directory on the Web, providing many budding writers a free venue to exhibit their product. Over twenty-five thousand writers submit content to *IdeaMarketers,* which allows individual writers to post articles to be featured on the site. Articles are stored in a searchable database where researchers, publishers, webmasters, and ezine editors can come in and find content.

As far as her own writing is concerned, her author friend, Marcia Lynn McClure, encouraged her to branch into fiction. She and Ms. McClure enjoy providing a new niche: clean romance novels. Since that time Marnie has written several novels integrating elements of the places, people, and events of her Southern family and heritage.

**What's next for Marnie Pehrson?** Marnie's latest passion is promoting an eclectic group of experts who specialize in everything from financial freedom to overcoming alcoholism to online marketing, small business, and real estate investing. The Expert Village at *IdeaMarketers* is fast becoming a bridge to those looking for specialized information and for media outlets to find qualified experts on varying topics.

You can reach Marnie Pehrson through:
www.pwgroup.com and www.ideamarketers.com

## Desiree Scales — CEO, Bella Web Design, Inc. and Advocate for Electronic Media

Desiree spent years with Delta Airlines, first as a flight attendant, then in corporate communications, where she became an expert at both intranet and Internet website development and operations. Later, to stay at home with her children, she launched Bella Web Design in 1998, a boutique Atlanta web design company that provides all the services needed for successful web-based media strategies, all in one place. During the next ten years, Bella Web Design grew, earning a #1 ranking on kudzu.com and over three hundred clients in thirty-five states.

In her work, Desiree began encountering more and more disillusioned people and businesses being taken advantage of, especially as the Internet usage exploded and electronic media expanded so fast. "I had heard so many horrible stories of web designers, database developers, hosting companies taking advantage of people over the last ten years. I'm saying this has got to stop, and it's got to stop right here." Today, Desiree's personal vision is to educate people and businesses so they don't fall into traps, can stop fearing the computer, and take a more active role in their online personality. She now speaks and advocates for people to understand the Internet and its uses, and learn to make educated decisions on their needs and uses of electronic media. "I want to share my knowledge and help people — it's like a bill of rights — here are your rights as a business owner for your website and what to expect."

**What's next for Desiree Scales?** Desiree plans to travel for speaking engagements, teaching and advocating for the Internet and its correct usage. She intends to help businesses and individuals learn about the new technologies they might use to enhance and promote their business and gain exposure. She also has plans for a book, to support the greatest possible audience.

You can reach Desiree through Bella Web Design: www.bellawebdesign.com or desiree@bellawebdesign.com

## Andrea Shelton, President — *Heartbound Ministries*

In 2000, Andrea Shelton's brother was in an auto accident. This began a long, arduous journey for him, which led to his being wrongly incarcerated for eighteen months before the situation was finally corrected and he was released. But, importantly, it set Andrea on a path to launch *Heartbound Ministries*, which is now directly involved with inmates in almost all of Georgia's prisons.

After visiting her brother for the first time in prison, and knowing his strong faith, she attempted to get him in touch with the prison's chaplain. It was then she learned that the state of Georgia was in the process of eliminating all the chaplains from the prison system due to budget cuts. Andrea, who also had a strong faith foundation, knew when her brother was sent to prison that something good would eventually come from all of this. As a lawyer from Georgia, with background experience with the state legislature, she went into action. Her vision became to save the chaplains in the state prisons, a vehicle of hope for so many inmates. This would lead her to the prisons themselves, a meeting with the governor of Georgia, and extensive advocacy on the chaplains' behalf, culminating in the creation of the nonprofit organization, *Heartbound Ministries*.

The mission of *Heartbound Ministries* is to serve and equip Georgia prison chaplains and minister to those in prison. Today the organization is a presence in almost every Georgia state and county prison and in about twenty-five youth facilities as well as many of the private prisons. They have gotten twenty chaplains returned to full-time status, and the remaining twenty-seven have been returned part-time to twenty-nine hours weekly.

Additionally, *Heartbound Ministries* advocates and supports the chaplains and the inmates through many efforts, including guest speakers such as professional athletes and others to share their stories, provide inspiration, and teach usable skills. They also provide items needed by the prisoners such as books, bibles, and personal products.

*Heartbound Ministries'* vision is to provide an alternative way of thinking to reduce the recidivism rates of these inmates. And it's working — three hundred and fifty inmates are released each month from prison, with roughly three out of four destined to return. But when inmates are involved in the chaplaincy faith-based programs, that recidivism rate drops from 73% to about 14%.

**What's next for Andrea Shelton?** Although Andrea has had requests to launch the program in other states, she feels her work in Georgia cannot be complete until all the chaplains are reinstated, full-time, throughout the system. Additionally, her organization now takes chaplains, wardens, and other prison personnel to the Louisiana State Penitentiary in Angola, LA twice a year — considered a model American prison. The hope is to inspire the vision and knowledge that they can impact their prisons in greater ways and, thus, make a positive difference in so many lives. She also continues to balance this unusual passion with her love of family, her husband and children.

You can reach Andrea and *Heartbound Ministries* through: ww.heartboundministries.org

## Barbara Stanny — Author, Speaker

Barbara grew up relying on her father (the "R" of H&R Block), then her husband, to manage her money. It wasn't until she suffered a personal devastating financial crisis that she woke up to her own responsibility regarding her finances.

Her journey to financial independence began by interviewing financially savvy women from diverse backgrounds. She discovered a surprising series of insights that all these women shared — insights that enabled them to feel "smart" about money. Those insights turned her life around, and became the core of her first book, *Prince Charming Isn't Coming: How Women Get Smart About Money.*

Her next step was to focus on women's earnings. For her next book, Barbara interviewed over one hundred and fifty women who make $100,000 or more. Her goal: to find out how they did it, if others could, too, and how to avoid the pitfalls along the way. From this new research came *Secrets of Six-Figure Women: Surprising Strategies to Up Your Earnings and Change Your Life.*

Barbara not only uncovered the secrets that enabled these women to become so financially successful, but personally proved her theory was possible. For the first time in her life, she became a six-figure woman, before she even finished writing the book.

Barbara's mission is to motivate women to become financially empowered. Her poignant experience with money gave her a unique perspective on women's financial issues. She has designed a powerful three-pronged approach to revolutionize a woman's relationship with money. Her books, workshops, coaching, and other products are based on these three components: 1) The Outer Work of Wealth™ (Practical), 2) The Inner Work of Wealth™ (Psychological), and 3) The Higher Work of Wealth™ (Personal & Philanthropic).

**What's next for Barbara Stanny?** To continue her mission, Barbara is doing the research on her next book, which will be about women who earn over a million dollars a year.

You can reach Barbara Stanny through:
www.barbarastanny.com

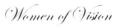

Barbara Stanny, Inc. / 2023 E Sims Way, Suite 328 / Port Townsend, WA 98368

## Margot Swann — Founder, *Visions Anew*

Margot took the first step on the journey to her passion one December day when her attorney husband of twenty years came home and told her he didn't want to be married to her any longer. Completely blindsided, Margot needed to find the resources to help her mentally, spiritually, and financially. Feeling both terrified and overwhelmed, she gathered a team of experts to help her navigate the divorce process and negotiate a financial settlement.

As a result of her experience, Margot developed a passion for sharing her knowledge and wisdom with other divorcing women. In 1998, she founded *Visions Anew Institute*, The Divorce Resource for Women. *Visions Anew* programs educate, support, and connect divorcing women with professionals, resources, and each other. Margot combines her skills as a Stephen's minister, divorce support facilitator, divorce coach, columnist, professional speaker, business owner, and seminar coordinator to create a space where divorcing women can create a new vision for their lives. Since then, this nonprofit organization has served thousands of women, positively impacting their lives as well as those of their ex-spouses and children.

**What's next for Margot Swann?** Today, in addition to her position as director of *Visions Anew Institute*, Ms. Swann is available to speak to groups and for private divorce coaching.

You can reach Margot Swann through:
www.visionsanew.org
Telephone: 770-953-2882

## Laura White — Founder, *Wild and Water*

Laura White is seventeen years old. She learned very early that not all kids her age can have and do the things she has been blessed with. During ninth grade that lesson became clear when she discovered her best friend was homeless and had been living in shelters. She realized that although they had so much in common and were the same in so many ways, her friend could not do the same things Laura could and did not have all the same opportunities she had heretofore taken for granted. Then, unexpectedly, her friend's family had to move to the other side of the country, and Laura was always worried about what had happened to her and how she was. This thought would motivate Laura to do something for other children in need in her own community.

An avid swimmer, Laura hoped to blend her own activities and find a way to provide them to others. She became concerned during a community-sponsored camping trip for disadvantaged eight-year-old children to Lake Alatoona. Everyone assumed the children could swim, but it became obvious very quickly when Laura had to jump in the lake and rescue five that they could not. She learned later about the lack of access to swimming lessons for disadvantaged children. She knew then that she had the experience and the drive to help. Her goals were to give children something to look forward to, something to do with their friends in a safe environment, to teach them swimming and life-saving skills, and also to provide fellow swimmers with volunteer opportunities. *Wild and Water* was born.

In July 2006, on her own initiative, she began organizing pool locations, donations of equipment, transportation, and volunteers to teach swimming lessons in the Atlanta area. The program proved to be so popular that *Wild & Water* was established as a nonprofit 501(c)3 organization to enlist community support and expand her program to additional cities and states to serve more children. Summer 2007 saw *Wild and Water* working with over one hundred and forty children at six facilities throughout Atlanta. In addition to school, swim meets, extracurricular activities, and SATs, Laura found herself running a foundation, fund-raising, organizing volunteers, and working with a board of directors.

Also, happily, Laura's best friend returned to Atlanta, and the two remain close.

**What's next for Laura White?** In addition to starting college in fall of 2008, Laura has created a partnership with the University of New Orleans to launch the program for children there, and is also in discussions to expand the program into Florida.

You can reach Laura through:
www.wildandwater.org

## Monica Willard — *United Religions Initiative,* United Nations NGO Representative

In 1985, Monica Willard took a wrong turn, or the right one as it turned out. A former teacher and family counselor, Monica was involving herself in community work after a decision to stay at home with her own children when her husband began traveling extensively. That day Monica was involved in an international art project, *Ribbons International,* through her work with the American Association of University Women. People and organizations were creating "ribbons," pieces of cloth of any form on which they would place what they could not bear to think would be lost forever in the event of a nuclear war. All kinds of formats were used, from needlepoint to paint and crochet — all visually demonstrating the hopes, dreams, and prayers of one person tied to another. The vision was to wrap this around the Pentagon on the fortieth anniversary of the bombing of Hiroshima, a gentle reminder to the Pentagon of what people could lose. Monica took her family down to Washington to find the New York ribbons and took a wrong turn, but ended up finding the ribbon she had made herself with her children's names. Standing there with her family, holding her ribbon and seeing what had been created, she told her husband, "You know I'm tied into this for life." The project became a non-governmental organization at the United Nations, and Monica joined them. This ultimately led her to the United Religions Initiative in 1991, where she has been working ever since, designing and organizing programs to further their goals.

*United Religions Initiative* was formed in order to have dialogue that reduces religiously motivated violence and to create cultures of peace and justice for the earth and all living things. It is different in that they started out as a grass roots organization, working not with religious leaders, but with people of varying faiths who wanted to work together to promote change. One such program Monica has been involved in for over fourteen years is the "Values Caucus," where ambassadors are invited in to discuss their ideas in a casual manner over coffee. It was here the then ambassador from Bangladesh gave a message about the "culture of peace." This became definitive terminology with the organization, and they have been striving since to represent this through public affairs and events. Monica herself works each year on programs for the UN's International Day of Peace, a yearlong planning cycle of events for adults, families, and children. It has become a mission in her life to promote a culture of peace. "I think culture in general is that thread that runs through and unites a society, and today we're living in a very global society."

**What's next for Monica Willard?** Monica continues her work with the United Nations. As she does every year, she is currently involved in the organization of the 2008 International Day of Peace and focused on educating the world that this day is held annually on September 21st. "One day of peace might not seem like much, however, if we can engage more and more people to choose peace in their daily actions and to have a shared focus to proclaim that peace is possible, this day observed annually will make a big contribution to creating world peace. Peace is possible if we choose it and live it!"

Monica is also now working with a number of organizations and UN Member States on a proposal to have the UN General Assembly proclaim a *Decade for Inter-religious Dialogue and Cooperation for Peace*.

You can reach Monica through:
www.uri.org and mbwillard@uri.org

## Serena Woolrich — Founder and Board Director, *Allgenerations*

Serena Woolrich loves people and enjoys helping them, no matter who they are. The daughter of a Holocaust survivor from Transylvania, Serena spent most of her adult life involved in a group known as *2^{nd} Generation* — sons and daughters of Holocaust survivors. While volunteering for this group in several cities, she began to see a need for an international information clearinghouse that could help survivors, their children, grandchildren, and friends with information or special needs. She began advocating for this and with the advent of the Internet began collecting email addresses of interested parties. Slowly, requests for assistance in locating relatives or for information began to appear, and *Allgenerations* began to grow. For years Serena ran this database and coordinated the searches in her own spare time, often spending thirty hours a week on top of her own full-time job in federal government.

Today *Allgenerations* has become a major international resource for survivors and their families, providing answers, assistance, support, and guidance for a diverse range of questions, current issues, or concerns. It is strictly an email program, unlike a club or chat room; it acts as a clearinghouse of information for matters of importance such as locating family members, healthcare, providing home visits, and helping indigent survivors. It has also become a resource for educators, historians, genealogists, authors, and filmmakers throughout the world involved with various aspects of the Holocaust. It provides education, historical studies, and documentation.

**What's next for Serena Woolrich?** *Allgenerations* became an official 501(c)3 in 2006, and Serena was able to retire from the federal government in 2007. She dedicates much of her time to *Allgenerations*, now with a membership over 1,300 She continues to maintain the database and use it to fulfill requests from survivors' families, as well as the Jewish and non-Jewish communities. Serena works more and more with educators, historians, and authors — developing connections for them around the world with survivors or others with valuable information. She also hosts events in several cities.

You can learn more about *Allgenerations*, learn of upcoming events, and contact Serena through:
www.allgenerations.com or allgenerations@aol.com

## Reverend Nancy Worth — Senior Minister, Unity North Atlanta

Reverend Nancy Worth will tell you that everything in life has a purpose and occurs perfectly, and she knows this through her own life experience. Whether it's money for a career change or the greater picture of life events leading her ultimately to her personal vision, everything in her life has unfolded perfectly.

Nancy started out after college as a professional dancer on and off Broadway. Later she became involved in newspaper publishing and met her husband. This would lead Nancy and her husband Bill to purchase and run a weekly paper on the island of Maui in Hawaii.

Perhaps the biggest turning point in Nancy's life occurred in 1986 while living in Hawaii. She had been involved in New Thought churches after college but had later fallen away from any religion. Yet, one morning Nancy suddenly had a desire to attend the local Unity church on the island of Maui and was disappointed to find that the minister she had anticipated hearing was not there. Instead they had a guest speaker named Wayne Dyer, and he spoke of a trip he was arranging to the Soviet Union. This trip would change the course of Nancy's life yet again.

That day was followed by an incredible series of events, beginning with the unexpected sale of Nancy and Bill's island newspaper and graphic arts company. This allowed her to join the group traveling to Russia for the *World Instant of Cooperation, World Peace Day,* a planetary affirmation of peace, love, forgiveness, and understanding involving millions of people in a simultaneous global link. Nancy discovered a passion for peace, and the trip set in motion a series of life changes for her, culminating in her returning to school at the Unity Institute in Missouri and becoming an ordained minister. Her husband, Reverend Bill Worth, would later follow her into the ministry, and they would work together in churches in Florida and Texas before Nancy became senior minister for Georgia's largest Unity church, Unity North Atlanta in 2005.

Nancy has a vision and believes if you have a vision you should tell people about it and bring it out. Her entire past provided her the necessary tools, knowledge, experience, and confidence to speak and reach people. And Reverend Nancy enjoys sharing her passion with others.

She enjoys ministry because spiritual community has become very important to her. "As we grow and transform, we help each other to do the same."

**What's next for Reverend Nancy Worth?** Reverend Nancy is nowhere near finished. She is so passionate about the Unity message she wants it to enrich everyone's life. Her dream now is to attract thousands and fill her church weekly. She plans to reach into her community more and more through media sources. Ultimately, her goal is to write a book and produce tapes to reach the largest possible audience.

Reverend Nancy can be reached through:
www.unitynorth.org

# Songs of Inspiration:
## Theme Songs from The Women Of Vision

Many of us find that music, and especially songs, hit a chord with us, inspiring us to dream big and follow our visions. These songs were given to us as those that inspire the women you have met within these pages:

| | |
|---|---|
| *Ain't Too Proud To Beg* | The Temptations |
| *I Did It My Way* | Frank Sinatra |
| *Amazing Grace* | Various Artists |
| *The Rose* | Bette Midler |
| *A Rose Is A Rose* | Susan Ashton |
| *I Can Only Imagine* | Mercy Me |
| *Many Different Roads* | Gladys Knight |
| *I Will Survive* | Gloria Gaynor |
| *Suddenly, I See* | KT Tunstall |
| *I Believe I Can Fly* | R. Kelly |
| *Let There Be Peace On Earth* | Various Artists |
| *One Moment In Time* | Whitney Houston |
| *Unwritten* | Natasha Bedingfield |
| *Be Thou My Vision* | Selah |
| *When You Wish Upon A Star* | Various Artists |
| *Eleanor Rigby* | The Beatles |
| *I Never Would Have Made It* | Marvin Sapp |
| *Will You Remember Me* | Sarah McLachlan |
| *Woman's Spirit* | Karen Drucker |
| *On My Way* | Karen Drucker |
| *Reach* | Gloria Estefan |
| *If I Were Brave* | Jana Stanfield |
| *When I Dream* | Karen Drucker |

# The Bridge Builder

By Will Allen Dromgoole

An old man, going a lone highway,
Came, at the evening, cold and gray,
To a chasm, vast, and deep, and wide,
Through which was flowing a sullen tide.
The old man crossed in the twilight dim;
The sullen stream had no fears for him;
But he turned, when safe on the other side,
And built a bridge to span the tide.
"Old man," said a fellow pilgrim, near,
"You are wasting strength with building here;
Your journey will end with the ending day;
You never again must pass this way;
You have crossed the chasm, deep and wide—
Why build you a bridge at the eventide?"
The builder lifted his old gray head:
"Good friend, in the path I have come," he said,
"There followeth after me today,
A youth, whose feet must pass this way.
This chasm, that has been naught to me,
To that fair-haired youth may a pitfall be.
He, too, must cross in the twilight dim;
Good friend, I am building the bridge for him."

139

# About The Authors

**Kathleen Smith**

A seasoned communications and marketing professional, Kathleen Smith worked more than twenty years in the entertainment and cultural arts industries, primarily for Disney Channel Worldwide and Woodruff Arts Center. These positions allowed her to indulge her passion for travel. She extensively explored the US and Europe, producing Disney Channel's *The Art of Disney Animation* and Woodruff's *Montreux Jazz Festival in Atlanta* (co-produced with Switzerland's Montreux Jazz Festival and the City of Atlanta). She has written articles and op-ed pieces, annual reports, foundation grant proposals, and many executive speeches.

Exciting as that was, she longed always to pen her own project. While working with The Disney Channel, she met her future writing partner, Liz Ireland, and they began searching for the right project to produce together. That "aha!" moment arrived in 2006 at a women's retreat in western Georgia. Soon after, Kathleen left her position as VP of Communications & Center Initiatives for Woodruff Arts Center and embarked on her own writing career. In addition to her writing projects, she currently consults on integrated communications and marketing programs for organizations in Atlanta. Kathleen believes that success is found in living passionately, producing prosperously, and always driving a convertible!

**Elizabeth Ireland**

Liz Ireland found her passion for the theater at an early age. After finishing graduate school, she embarked upon a career as an instructor in the Performing Arts Center of a liberal arts college in northern Illinois. For ten years Liz taught, directed, and managed house operations for a vibrant performing arts program and wrote or re-wrote a number of plays. She lived, breathed, and celebrated in her theatrical life. Soon after receiving tenure and an associate professorship, she took a well-deserved sabbatical and discovered her passion was no longer in the theater. Her real passion was for writing. She turned her talents to screenwriting, eventually writing and collaborating on fifteen screenplays. Two of her own scripts were semi-finalists in the *Don and Gee Nicholl Fellowship* in screenwriting sponsored by the Academy of Motion Picture Arts and Sciences, while four others were optioned, but remain unproduced. While working at Disney Channel Worldwide, she met a soul sister in Kathleen, and the two began a quest for their project.

After coming up with and subsequently discarding numerous creative projects, they finally formulated the *Women of Vision* project in 2006. The result has brought them both great joy as well as unbound enthusiasm for all the wonderful women they have encountered along the way.

Today Liz is primary caregiver for her ninety-three-year-old mother-in-law and beautiful adopted eleven-year-old Chinese daughter. She now sees herself as the heroine in her *own* comedy-adventure film.

Printed in the United States
125286LV00002B/28-45/P